LOVE IN THE AGE OF VAMPIRISM

"The first time he drank my blood we were having sex and he asked if he could cut me. At first I felt uncomfortable, but it really was an incredible experience. He let me drink from him and it was magical. I felt—I sometimes still do—closer to him than anyone I'd ever known. It was the most intimate experience I've ever had. . . . Even though I haven't loved anyone since then, I hope to find a partner I can share this with again. Since then, I have had the cravings for blood a few times. When this happens I simply cut my arm and drink my own blood. It brings back the memories, which always makes me cry."

Yes, they *are* really out there. . . .

"An oddly interesting, quirky excursion."   —Booklist

BLOOD LUST

CONVERSATIONS WITH REAL VAMPIRES

CAROL PAGE

A DELL BOOK

Published by
Dell Publishing
a division of
Bantam Doubleday Dell Publishing Group, Inc.
666 Fifth Avenue
New York, New York 10103

Lyrics for "Undead," "Rise," and "Lord of the Damned" copyright ©
TDT Music, and are used here by permission.

ISBN: 0-440-21393-2

Reprinted by arrangement with HarperCollins, Publishers

Printed in the United States of America

Published simultaneously in Canada

October 1992

10 9 8 7 6 5 4 3 2 1

OPM

To
Bill T. Miller and O'Brien,

and in memory of
Miss Grace.

ACKNOWLEDGMENTS

Molly Friedrich, my agent, offered her energy, support, and vision. Craig Nelson, my editor, gave his support, superb judgment, and humor. Nick Allison provided top-notch, careful copyediting. Bill T. Miller, my sweet baby, supplied his usual unconditional loyalty and love, in addition to a lot of fantastic ideas. Larry Hitt transcribed tapes, critically read and edited copy, and generally cheered me along. His help was essential.

Matthew Christian provided interest and support, putting his prize-winning beefy boy body on the line more than once as bodyguard and researcher. Dr. Jeanne Youngson, president of the Count Dracula Fan Club, generously provided me with information and time whenever I needed it. Dr. Robert S. McCully, Ph.D., critically read transcripts of my interviews with various vampires and provided professional insights concerning their behavior and what they said about themselves. So did Linda Barbanel, M.S.W., who kindly took breaks from being the Dr. Ruth of money to think about blood drinking and what it means. Dr.

Katherine Ramsland also read transcripts of interviews and provided valuable insights, as well as other practical assistance, for which I am most grateful. Dr. Raymond McNally offered his knowledge and assistance and opinions, which I respect and value. Eric Held, of the Vampire Information Exchange Network, helped with hard-to-find books and other valuable information. His newsletter was an essential source for contacts.

I also want to thank Andre Ryan; Jane Ehrlich; Marianna Beck; Sarah Koolsbergen; Mary Frakes; Fleur Brennan; attorneys Willie Davis and Fran Robinson; Allen J. Gittens; Robert James-Leake; Julia Kruk; Carole Bohanan; Lewis Harrison; John Joslyn; James Randi and Barry Karr of the Committee for the Scientific Investigation of the Claims of the Paranormal; Dr. Russel Tomar, professor of pathology at the University of Wisconsin Hospital and Clinics; Virgin Atlantic Airlines; Patrick Arton of Lou Hammond & Associates; the Crown Hotel in Scarborough; Chad Savage; Paul and Lincoln Barrett; Teresa Simmons of the Anne Rice/Vampire Lestat Fan Club; Jim Mittaeger; Dorothy Nixon; William Strockbine, registrar at SUNY-Stony Brook; as well as all the vampires who told me their stories. If I forgot anybody, I'm sorry.

BLOOD LUST

INTRODUCTION

*T*he average American child doesn't get very far in life without meeting a vampire. He may eat Count Chocula cereal—chocolate-flavored cereal vampires mixed with marshmallow bats—for breakfast, pasta vampires and bats for lunch, and fruit-flavored vampire- and bat-shaped fruit chews as an afternoon snack. He may eat this snack while learning to count from the charming Muppet called the Count on Sesame Street, who counts everything in sight, laughing happily as he does, his little companion bats fluttering around him. In fact, an average American child may have a Count doll or puppet at home. On Saturday morning, she may watch Count Duckula cartoons, a series about a good-natured vegetarian vampire duck who does not want to drink blood, despite the encouragement of his ghoulish nanny and butler. Or she may read the Bunnicula children's books about a vampire bunny rabbit.

Throughout the year, this child may see half a dozen commercials featuring vampires. One vampire refuses to pay a lot for his muffler. A toy vampire, after rising from his coffin, is still flying on two-year-old batteries. Vampires have been used to advertise candy bars, booze, hair products, pesticides, mouthwash, gum, cat food, bananas, pizza, nail polish, security systems, computer software, and cars, among many other products. The child may see vampire episodes of regular television series such as *The Monkees, Superboy,* and *Trapper John, M.D.* If he's lucky, he may run across reruns of the famous vampire soap opera, "Dark Shadows."

As the child grows older, he may become interested in comic books, in which vampires have long been portrayed, most recently with a version of Anne Rice's Lestat. This average American child is likely to become interested in horror films, where, alongside Freddy and other modern monsters, the classic horror figure of the vampire is frequently seen. Elvira, Mistress of the Dark, will show him some of the older vampire films, while new films are continually being made for television, the theaters, and the video market. Since the interest in vampires is currently so strong, George Hamilton has plans to make the sequel to probably the most popular vampire comedy ever made, *Love at First Bite.* Even Bo Derek plans to appear as Countess Dracula in an upcoming film.

Later, as his or her reading skills improve, an average child may start reading vampire fiction, including Bram Stoker's novel *Dracula,* which stands as the beginning of the huge industry that the vampire has become, an industry of books, films, comic books, records, television shows, costumes, and memorabilia. Every year dozens of new fictional vampire books are published. Most popular is the vampire trilogy of author Anne Rice, *Interview with the Vampire, Vampire Lestat,* and *Queen of the Damned.*

By now this average American child has seen fake blood dripping down the chins of Alice Cooper, Nikki Sixx, and Ozzy Osbourne in videos on MTV or live on stage. Rock-and-roll and vampires go hand in hand, as Anne Rice showed when she made her vampire Lestat into a rock star. Both are outsider worlds which beckon with promises of danger, romance, and power.

Should this hypothetical child not get much exposure to popular culture, she surely has not been able to escape noticing Halloween, when the novelty and greeting-card industries deluge us with vampires. Dozens of vampire Halloween cards appear each Halloween, some with cute, cuddly child vampires, others with frightening, monstrous vampires, and yet others with sexy vampires offering romantic or even blatantly sexual messages.

One shows a drawing of a city with a few bats flying around and reads, "This is the city. Transylvania. A million people lie in bed or sit staring out a castle window, waiting for the fog to lift. Sometimes, one of them gets the urge to rise and bite someone on the neck. That's when I go to work. My name's Friday—" Inside, the card reads, "I carry a stake."

Another shows a vampire in a coffin, and a man standing over him with a hammer, saying, "Quick, Smedley, it's nearly sunset. Give me the stake! Smedley, the stake!" Smedley is picking up a sirloin and the caption reads, "Smedley makes a mistake." Inside, the message is, "Count on me to get to the heart of the matter."

Yet another shows a cartoon vampire with a blanket wrapped around another smiling cartoon character, with a caption reading, "It's Halloween." Inside: "Suck someone you love."

The vampire has shown up in political cartoons lately, too. One done by Steve Kelley of the *San Diego Union* shows Gorbachev in a hospital with a chart labeled SOVIET ECONOMY at the foot of his bed. Uncle Sam is visiting and Gorbachev is saying, "Oh, Sam, when you get a minute, I could use a transfusion." Uncle Sam is unable to respond, since a vampire, labeled "S&Ls," is sinking his teeth into Sam's neck.

In a political cartoon by Victor Juhasz, President Bush, dressed in army fatigues and carrying a stake and mallet, is approaching Manuel Noriega, who is dressed in a vampire's cape and is crouched in a corner. But it is Noriega who is holding up a cross, a reference to his period of refuge in the residence of the Panamanian representative of the Vatican.

The vampire is one of the most popular choices for Halloween costumes, particularly the traditional Dracula costume with red-lined cape, black hair, white makeup, and fangs. Fangs come in many varieties, including twenty-five-cent plastic fangs that bend to cover the front upper and lower teeth, glow-in-the-dark versions, and wax ones. Expensive dentist-made fangs, some removable, some not, are worn by those who are serious about their costumes, the ones who always win the contest. Fake blood comes in many varieties, soft capsules that can be bitten for a particularly gruesome effect or in convenient tubes and squeeze bottles. Alternatively, dressing as one of the vampire Lost Boys has become popular since that film was released. For those who like to be really scary, rubber Nosferatu masks are available.

In early October, candy bars appear on the counters

of convenience stores, Count Crunch, Creepy Coffin, and Vampbite, each wrapped in foil printed with a colorful, fanged cartoon vampire. Next to them are little plastic coffins filled with bone-shaped candies. Marked down in November, they eventually disappear until the following year. Pricier candy stores offer high-quality chocolate bats on sticks.

Paper garlands of bats, tablecloths, napkins, and paper plates adorned with bats, even plastic cocktail toothpicks with bats become available, along with rubber bats in many varieties. Fuzzy stuffed bats appear in the stores, too; push the belly of one model, and its eyes light up red and it emits a scary Halloween whine. Others squeak when squeezed. Vampire windup toys are available—everything from a caped vampire who scoots across the floor to a vampire head whose mouth opens and closes. Vampire snow domes in which bats, instead of snow, fly around in the water while a pale, white hand slides aside the top of a tomb appear in normally conservative Hallmark stores, next to pins of a vampire in which the red eyes, powered by a small battery, flash on and off.

So-called vampire cats dressed in capes are trotted out on Regis Philbin's show. Halloween is always the season for Drs. Radu Florescu and Raymond McNally to appear on talk shows and tell about the inspiration for Count Dracula, their scholarly subject of choice, the Rumanian prince Vlad Tepes. The doctors have managed to maintain their dignity and scholarly reputation while doing so.

The tabloid press knows that their readers love a good vampire story, and the *Weekly World News* and the *National Examiner* provide them regularly. The *Weekly World News* ran a wonderful story about one

Peter Vlahuta, a Rumanian businessman who claimed to be a descendant of Vlad Tepes, who leads a gang of "bloodsuckers" in Sumatra, biting and killing beautiful young girls. Of course, not a word of it is true. MY GARLIC BREATH SAVED ME FROM VAMPIRE WOMAN is another *Weekly World News* headline. In this story, an American businessman visiting Bucharest was nearly seduced by a vampiress. Fortunately, he had eaten lamb stew that evening which had been strongly flavored with garlic. When she tried to bite him in the neck, he opened his mouth and gasped in her face, so disgusting her that she rushed away into the night.

Count Dracula first appeared upon the popular culture scene in the 1890s. He didn't make that big a splash; in fact, his creator, Bram Stoker, died a pauper. Although vampire stories appeared before and after Stoker's book, it wasn't until Bela Lugosi took up his cape that Dracula became a household word. Lugosi's unintentionally camp portrayals of the count remain popular today and curiously fascinating.

In the late sixties, an offbeat vampire soap opera appeared on American televisions, heralding an important change in the way vampires were viewed. Soon kids were rushing home from school so that they could see *Dark Shadows*. The show lasted for five years, and gained a large cult following; committed fans hold conventions to this day. Their loyalty paid off; the soap opera was revived as a prime-time series with a new cast. The show was important because it showed a vampire as a human being with needs and loves and pain, about which he spoke most articulately. Barnabas was not just a monster; his sufferings drew a new, large audience, many of them women who hadn't previously been especially interested in vampires.

When Frank Langella played Dracula on Broadway and then again in film, he further humanized the vampire, making him even more attractive to a much larger audience by emphasizing the intensely erotic side of the character. Although the film was not a major box office success, vampires and sex were now firmly linked in the public mind.

The passionate and erotic books of Anne Rice brought the vampire firmly into the present. Her rebellious, anguished Lestat captured the imagination of many readers who had no previous interest in vampires, and the strong sales of Rice's books have led to a new deluge of vampire books, movies, and television shows that may very well make the nineties—as Rice's biographer, Dr. Katherine Ramsland, has suggested—the decade of the vampire.

Dark Shadows, Langella's Dracula, and Anne Rice's novels have sparked a newfound passion for an old monster by transforming him into a modern-day fantasy figure, one that fits the bill when it comes to the kinds of fantasies needed by bored, stressed-out Americans. They gladly escape into the fantasy of darkness, where exquisite men and women live in a world of power, wealth, and a rich yet perverse knowledge that comes from being very, very old.

For some, the appeal is in the darkness itself. Night people are temperamentally quite different from people who love bright sunshine. Many night people say they feel relieved when night finally comes, when the world is no longer so loud and intense. Distracting, ugly details disappear in the darkness. One is better able to focus on the moment, the immediate sensations of touch and taste, sound and smell. Now the night people can take off their suits, leaving their computer terminals and department-store perfume counters behind, and put on their silks or leathers and pursue satisfaction and pleasure.

For the majority of vampire aficionados, the appeal is romantic and sexual. Dracula overwhelms his victim, and that is the most important aspect of his sexual appeal. That so many men and women are drawn to a figure with such overwhelming sexual power may indicate that a kind of backlash is taking place. After two decades of earnest discussion about relationships and simultaneous orgasms, after careful examination of every motivation to make sure that no one is being exploited, after all that honesty and sharing, many people are concluding that they also want hot sex, the groaning, screaming kind that completely empties the mind of anything but the two turned-on bodies. In fact, that's all they ever wanted.

Phil Donahue and Alan Alda, most often named as quintessential liberated men, just don't seem to offer such promises. The fantasy figure of Dracula, who can now conveniently be given the face of Frank Langella or David Bowie, does offer such overwhelming possibilities. In fantasy, it is possible to take things as far as one wants and no further. Dracula takes his victim into his powerful arms, looking into her eyes with his own deeply mesmerizing gaze. He is so compelling that it is impossible to look away. She is overwhelmed. She has no control. Night has come, and she has no choice but to abandon herself to the powerful vampire.

Frank Langella received a lot of heat when he made this comment about his role as Dracula: "I can't think of a woman who wouldn't like to be taken if it's with love. If you take a woman by force and at the same time gently, you can't go wrong." Langella isn't talking about rape, he's talking about sexual abandon.

The bite is in reality a passionate kiss that has broken the skin, leaving a bruise to cover with a scarf, which is removed back at the computer terminal only for an occasional peek so as to remember the night of passion. The infection of vampirism that Dracula passes with his bite is, in fantasy, falling in love, falling in love so deeply that one's life has changed forever, transformation through passion.

Men want to be overwhelmed in this way, too. University of Missouri psychologists William Arndt, Jr., John Foehl, and Elaine Good did a study on the sexual content of daydreams and found that 87 percent of men daydreamed about a woman "forcing her intentions" on him, or getting a woman "so excited that she screams with pleasure." It's not a personal matter of one individual dominating another or the kind of intimidating personal power that reduces one partner, making him or her less, inferior. No doubt these men would like to be screaming with pleasure, too.

Of course, people who have strong submissive or dominant tendencies are often fascinated by the vampire myth, too, and incorporate a version of it into their sexual practices. Dr. Jeanne Youngson, president of the Count Dracula Fan Club, has been hearing from vampire fans for twenty-five years, and consistently receives letters from women in their teens who beg to be introduced to a vampire, so that they can be seduced and bitten. Some practitioners of sadomasochism carry their practices to the extremes of bloodletting and blood drinking. Most say they do it because it is so sexually arousing, but some dominant practitioners say that they feel powerful, like Dracula, when they lick the blood off the whipped backs of their victims.

Power is another important reason people are so fascinated by the vampire. Dracula has deep, hypnotic eyes and can put his victims into a trance that causes them to lose their will. Some authors have given the vampire telepathic ability; he can call people to him with his mind, or he can cause them to forget what has happened or become confused, so as to not inter-fere with his activities.

The potential of such power is appealing to contem-plate. Imagine being able to, for example, flick one's fingers and cause your boss to say, "Well, yes, of course I'll double your salary. No, wait, I'll triple it," or meeting a handsome man in a club and easily being able to cause him to fall in love with you and follow your will.

Vampire buffs are also fascinated by the vampire's immortality. While Dracula was one of the undead, many modern films and books describe vampires as a separate race that has lived in the shadows since the beginning of time. For some, the idea of immortality is very attractive, even if it means never seeing sun-light and killing others in order to drink their blood. "I'd choose my victims very carefully," one vampire fan said, when asked if he would become a vampire if he could. "I'd only kill conservatives."

It is a complicated moral dilemma. The unnamed vampire in the film *Dance of the Damned* chose his victim because, through telepathy, he knew she wanted to die. Rice's Lestat usually chooses his vic-tims from the criminal element, in part because they won't be missed, but also because he presumes to serve as judge, jury, and executioner.

Others aren't so sure immortality is that appealing. "Oh, no," one fan replied. "That means I'd have to keep coming up with the rent forever." Of course, most fictional vampires tend to be very wealthy, either from nighttime criminal activities, made easier by their superhuman strength and ability to sense the presence of others (such as security guards), or from, as the vampire in *Dance of the Damned* put it, "long-term investments."

For many vampire fans, though, the idea of immortality is the part of the vampire myth that is most thrilling. The choice would not be what to do, but in what order. There's enough time to learn the harpsichord, raise parrots, study botany, live in Rome or Rio or Bangkok, paint, sculpt, or write, to do everything—except watch the sunrise over the Sahara or lie on the beach on Mykonos. Is the price worth paying? Many say yes. Still, fictional vampires do go mad from the sheer weight of eternity on their shoulders, jumping into the fire, one of the few ways that they can be killed.

The idea of immortality is particularly appealing to Americans, who have been, for the past two decades in particular, urgently obsessed with youth and beauty. Vampires do not age; rather, they live forever at whatever age they were when they were "turned." Many people would find it quite wonderful to be physically frozen at the age of eighteen and at their lowest adult weight of 108 pounds. With the exception of Bela Lugosi, who was almost comically ugly, most television and film vampires, as well as the more popular literary vampires of the past twenty years, are attractive people, a very important aspect of the appeal of the vampire in the nineties.

Blood drinking, in myth and reality, has a long history, and stories of vampirism have appeared throughout the world. Blood, after all, is the essence of life, and not just symbolically. Loss of blood leads to weakness, and it was no great leap of logic for early man, however incorrectly, to conclude that drinking blood would give him strength. This instinctual effort to cure illness, although undocumented, may have been the earliest example of vampirism.

The blood covenant is a form of blood drinking that appears in many cultures. The nineteenth-century explorer Henry Morton Stanley exchanged blood with many African tribal chiefs, each drinking a few drops of the blood of the other to seal the covenant. An alternative method developed by the Kayans of Borneo involved mixing the blood of the participants with tobacco, which was then rolled into a cigar and smoked.

In the Mahabharata, an epic poem which forms the basis of Hinduism, warriors speak of drinking the blood of their vanquished enemies from their skulls, and, after doing so, one warrior says, "The blood of my enemy tastes sweeter than my mother's milk." The ancient Gauls drank the blood of their dead enemies, as did the Sioux Indians, and the Burgundians drank the blood of the fallen in a great battle in the burning hall of the Huns in A.D. 437, according to the German epic the *Nibelungenlied*.

The Moche of Peru ritually drank the blood of their prisoners in ceremonial goblets, probably mixing *ulluchu*, an ancient fruit of the papaya family, with the blood to prevent coagulation. For some warriors, drinking the blood of their enemies was the ultimate act of vengeance, but many believed that the courage and strength of their enemies could be absorbed through this ritual. As recently as 1971, a member of the Black September organization who supposedly assassinated Wasfi Tal, the prime minister of Jordan, was quoted as saying, "I am satisfied now. I drank from Tal's blood," a claim confirmed by witnesses.

The blood of executed criminals was thought to have great power. In West Africa and among the Shans of Burma, the executioner would drink a small amount of the blood of the executed person, to protect himself from being possessed by the ghost of the man he had killed. In nineteenth-century China, the blood of decapitated criminals was soaked up in balls of bread and sold as medicine.

Arnald of Villanova, a thirteenth-century physician, astrologer, and alchemist, distilled blood to make what he believed was a medicine of great power against all diseases. The complicated recipe involved collecting blood from healthy, ruddy-cheeked, hot-tempered men during the months of April and May. The blood was distilled repeatedly, with the juices of flowers and fruits added. Arnald claimed that he gave the special blood medicine to a count thought to be dead, who revived for an entire hour, long enough for him to make his last confession. The dying Louis XI of France drank the blood of children in the hope of recovering.

The Mau Maus used blood drinking in their oath-taking ceremonies which, common in African ritual, had great power in establishing loyalty among members. Generally the blood of slaughtered animals was used, although a small amount of the initiates' own blood was also involved. For oaths required of persons of a higher rank, ghastly, murderous blood-drinking ceremonies were required, involving the blood of an adult and a child killed especially for the rites.

Isiah Oke, a former juju high priest in West Africa, devotes a large part of his book *Blood Secrets: The True Story of Demon Worship and Ceremonial Murder* to descriptions of the many voodoo rituals involving the drinking of both animal and human blood. In an important initiation ceremony, Oke was required to drink deeply of the blood of a rooster and a baby leopard. Blood rituals are a part of almost everybody's spiritual life in Africa, for animism is widely practiced there, even among supposedly converted Christians. Human blood is commonly used in these rituals, too, and Oke suggests that these practices may be at least partly responsible for the high incidence of AIDS in Africa.

The notorious Baby Doc Duvalier, upon leaving Haiti, is said to have sacrificed several unbaptized babies and drunk their blood in a voodoo ritual to ensure that the new government would fail. Special blood-drinking bowls are kept in voodoo temples, not unlike the practice of one group of vampires in this book who keep a set of cheap dime-store stemware for their vampirism.

Vampires do live among us. It is unlikely that they exist as a separate race, with supernatural powers. The nature of these vampires—as supernatural beings, or people infected with a virus, or people with porphyria, or simply mentally ill people who latch onto the vampire myth in an effort to become powerful—has been examined by authors and filmmakers for years. Are they descendants of Cain? Is vampirism connected to rabies or the plague? Is it a genetic mutation?

Vampires are simply people who drink blood. There are about as many reasons for drinking blood as there are vampires, but generally the reasons fall into two categories: intimacy and power. Vampires are not three hundred years old while appearing to be only twenty. The blood they drink has no effect on them physiologically. It does not keep them young and they do not physically need it, although some vampires believe they do. It doesn't make them high, except psychologically, or give them nutrition, since human blood passes through the digestive system without being absorbed. They do not have superhuman strength. They cannot turn into bats and wolves. Some sleep in coffins during the day and dress in black capes or indulge in other affectations inspired by fictional vampires.

The vampires you will meet in this book are all in their twenties or thirties. Except for one, they do not claim to be hundreds of years old. If you were sitting next to any of these people at a party, it would be impossible to tell that they were blood drinkers. Several are artists, one is a rock musician, another works in corrections, another does cleaning jobs. One is in prison for murder.

Once has been diagnosed as a paranoid schizophrenic. Another has had problems with depression. Others clearly have psychiatric problems that have not been diagnosed because of their duplicity in speaking with mental health professionals by whom they have been interviewed. Some have used drugs, including cocaine, heroin, marijuana, alcohol, and steroids. Most have had difficult, even terrible, childhoods, although not everybody cares to characterize his or her childhood that way. Several are intelligent, talented, and likable people.

Real-life blood drinkers have never been scientifically studied by qualified medical researchers. Most vampires keep their activities a secret because they don't want to end up in a mental hospital. Samples of their blood have never been analyzed, and medical and psychiatric histories have never been taken and statistically compared. A serious scientific study of these people would be intensely interesting, and might reveal a common denominator that would help to explain why some people have the urge to drink blood, and determine whether medical treatment would help them. Anemia is common among the vampires in this book, although not all are anemic. A few have other, more unusual blood conditions. Some have no known medical problems, at least none involving their blood.

Some of these vampires were aware of the urge to drink blood from early childhood. For others, the desire came along at puberty. For still others, it happened by chance, the result of crossing paths with other blood drinkers. Some of them were strongly influenced by vampire books and movies, while others developed their desire to drink blood independent of such influences. If these particular vampires have anything in common at all, it's their willingness to break a taboo, and their unwillingness to consider their blood drinking undesirable behavior that should be stopped.

CHAPTER 1

*People don't want you to drink blood. They want you to
drink Nescafé, preferably decaf.*

—JACK

He's tall and big. He works out,
but has gone about as far as he should, or his head
will start looking too small for his body. He'll continue
to work out, of course. He's quite a hunk, in fact, a
muscle boy with dark brown hair in a marine cut. His
sexual charisma is powerful. Both men and women,
upon meeting Jack, have felt the urge to wrap their
legs around his waist. The leather pants and inten-
tional rip in his T-shirt help.

His teeth are white and even, his smile kind and
disarming. In fact, he's rather a gentle giant in manner
and appearance. His voice is deep and booming—he
could do radio, but for his tone, which is flat, making
him sound unsure of himself, or even a little dumb,
even when he's not talking about drinking blood.

"I think I was born a vampire," Jack began. One of
his earliest memories is from around the age of four.

He would allow mosquitoes to light on him and then watch, fascinated, as they filled up with his blood. It drove his mother crazy. She would slap the mosquitoes away and yell at him.

Ten kids in a two-bedroom trailer led to shared beds, and it was with one of his brothers that he discovered his bisexuality. Jack liked to bite his brother. He didn't draw blood, although he did draw the blood to the surface of his brother's skin where he could just taste it, which is what a hickey really is. "I didn't want to hurt him," he said, "but I felt as though I got something from him when I did it. I enjoyed that. It's an odd feeling—well, it's not odd for me." He wasn't interested in hurting his brother and he "never tasted the bittersweet," his term for actually drinking blood. Still, Jack feels that he got "a lot of his feelings, some of his ideas," from his brother when he sucked so fiercely on him.

His brother didn't seem to mind; in fact, Jack says he was willing. "It was a very intense moment for both of us," he said. "I feel as though us being actual brothers had a lot to do with it, too. Why I went as far as I did. But I'm unsure of that.

"I'm learning," he went on. "I'm constantly learning about this whole situation with me. And I'm not as scared anymore. I was scared of the unknown. Scared of not knowing or how to tell people what I was. Scared of just not being able to put how I felt in words and scared of people not accepting that."

Jack has good reason to be scared. It's not easy being a vampire. People who drink blood—whether they are born with what they feel is a genuine physical need for it, or they fall into it, perhaps through some sexual experience—often find that desire to be very powerful. It doesn't go away, even though months or even years can pass without any activity. It's often an obsession. As Lestat will tell you in Anne Rice's wonderful vampire novels, the tension, the desire, the hunger, the need is always there, more intense at some times than at others perhaps, but always, always there.

Getting that blood can be difficult. Suppose someone cuts her finger while chopping mushrooms and her vampire friend across the kitchen, busy swirling lettuce in the salad spinner, feels a strong desire to suck the blood from her friend's injured finger and, when the friend goes for a Band-Aid, perhaps to carefully lick the blood from the knife, too. But she doesn't, she can't, she stifles the strong impulse, because her mushroom-chopping friend doesn't know about her secret, that she's a vampire.

If she did yield to that powerful impulse, the chances are very high that her friend would be horrified, even sickened by it. A friendship could end, and has, over a little mushroom-chopping accident.

Jack said it beautifully: "People don't want you to drink blood. They want you to drink Nescafé, preferably decaf."

Since the urge to drink blood is very powerful for most vampires, it has to be examined and even acted upon, or else it hovers around the edges of their consciousness, interfering with their peace of mind, never giving them complete rest. The need to express what Jack calls "vampire tendencies" is strong, but the trick is to express them in a way that "doesn't scare themselves and the people around them."

They find each other. Instead of yielding to the impulse to suck the blood from her friend's cut finger, a vampire will find other vampires and donors, people who are willing to give them blood. That's how most vampires get the blood they want or believe they need —from willing donors. Some donors do it out of love, to help the vampire, especially if the vampire genuinely believes he or she needs the blood to stay strong and well, even to live.

Some donors do it because it's kinky, crazy, fun, wild. Many do it because it's hot. Allowing someone else to drink your blood during sex is very exciting, if you like that kind of thing. There's the cut or the piercing or the bite, whatever is done to break the skin. *My God,* the vampire thinks, although probably not consciously, *I really have power over this person. I turn them on incredibly. Look what they're willing to do for me.* In the midst of all the sweat and heat comes a small cut with a sharp razor blade or a knife—X-Acto, paring, or Swiss army, they've all been used. A small amount of pain, not a lot, the amount most people can tolerate and many people like, and then the sharp smell of blood. It's a dark, rich, appetizing red, and the vampire and his donor become even more turned on as they watch it flow. The heat, the flesh, the blood, the intimacy, the power—this is consciousness-altering sex. This is hotter than hot.

Jack said he just knows when he crosses paths with a fellow vampire. The first time was when he was a freshman in high school. "I met this person, and when I first met him I knew. His name was Paul, and I just knew. Even upon seeing him, I didn't know exactly what I knew, but I knew it. We became very good friends, and we were in gym class. One day, we were playing soccer out on the field and we came in and he had fallen down. He had scraped his knee and was bleeding. And he looked at me, and through the eye contact, I knew.

"He was sitting on a bench in the locker room. We both lingered, because we had to wait for the other people to get out. And then I just, I drank from his knee. I knew. I knew. It's something that I couldn't even begin to explain."

Paul was comforted when Jack settled his hungry mouth on his torn-up knee. "It wasn't a comfort that a Band-Aid would bring," he added. "I never do this in front of people who I feel would be offended. In the world we live in today, you can get a title put on you too quickly for some of the things you do."

Like *vampire*. Jack doesn't like the word *vampire* because it immediately conjures up images of capes, Hungarian accents, coffins, and fangs. "A vampire to everybody else is that little guy right there," he said, pointing to a doll of the Muppet character called the Count, perched on top of a Mexican armadillo mask hung near my desk. "I don't really even like the color black. That's not where it's at. I do things out of instinct. I don't consider myself weird."

Jack found drinking from Paul's knee to be "very natural." Although he called it drinking, the actual amount of blood that he got was very small, and generally when Jack drinks blood, he doesn't drink much, a couple of ounces at most. Why would a fourteen-year-old boy sink to his knees in front of an injured schoolmate and suck blood from his knee? Jack became visibly excited as he tried to explain it to me. He very much wanted me to understand.

"It's almost like a baby trying to tell you why he wants his mother's nipple. It's such an instinct that it cannot be explained. Like I said, you can get a feel for it, but that is me and that was him. To actually say a reason for it would be so hard other than purely instinct. Purely instinct. I knew. His eyes told me. I knew."

That wasn't the only time Jack mentioned drinking from mother's breast. Paul allowed Jack to drink his blood again. "At one time, he slit his breast," Jack explained. That's Jack's body area of choice, at least when it comes to drinking blood, although he has even drunk blood out of somebody's foot, which he found quite erotic. Most people cut themselves for him in the area of their nipples and he simply says it's because "a man sucked his mother's breast. I am attracted to the breast because that is a human instinct I was born with. I still have those instincts that any other child would have."

Jack's need to connect and know a person can be so strong that he will literally drink that person's blood to feel close. With nine siblings in clearly a poor family, he probably didn't get much love or attention from his mother. Feeling that your mommy doesn't love you can do terrible things to a person. Jack swore that he and his mother love each other very much, and are very close, calling her "the dearest person in the world to me. I can't explain my love for her." But there was something suspicious in his insistence on this ideal mother. Some months after our interview, when Jack's family found out he was gay, no one in his family would talk to him, including his beloved mother.

Jack is bisexual actually, but with a strong preference for men, and he has never drunk a woman's blood. "I don't have as strong of a desire to, either. With some I do, but there is a very strong desire for me to drink a man's blood," he told me.

Vampires haven't been studied much, not seriously, except for those few who went off the deep end and attacked or even murdered someone. If a vampire ends up in a psychiatrist's office, it's usually because he was discovered and forced to go there. It's not something you should admit to, lest you find yourself in a straitjacket being hustled by men in white coats to the van for a ride to the mental hospital. Many psychologists have a tendency to try to fit human behavior into a rigid framework, rather than allow people to be who they are. A lot of them just won't believe it when their patients tell them they're vampires. It's unlikely that any psychiatrists consider vampirism an acceptable alternative lifestyle, although most vampires do.

Jack says that drinking blood gives him great pleasure. "It's happiness," he said. Jack's voice soared and nearly broke as he told me, "It is like making love. It's like the orgasm. It is the most inwardly erotic, sensual, warm, spiritual, uplifting thing that I do in my life. It gives me goose bumps to really express it.

"It's wow. It's heaven. That is heaven to me."

"More so than anything else?" I asked.

"More so," Jack replied.

"More so than sexual orgasm?" I pressed.

"Oh. Oh." Jack groaned. The man was really blissing out; there was nothing phony about it. "Drinking blood compared to orgasms is like the Pacific compared to a drop in the bucket. And I enjoy sexual orgasms. Oh, yes. I get so happy talking about it. It's incredible, Carol. I thank whoever instilled this in me. I thank them sincerely with my life," he said.

Jack feels very strongly, though, about not hurting anyone in the process. In fact, he does not cut or bite or in any way break the skin of any of his donors. They must always do it themselves, to demonstrate their willingness to give him their blood.

"It's not that it would bother me. My father was a poacher and I saw him slice deer open. It doesn't bother me to see blood. But it would bother me to cut someone if I wanted to drink that person's blood. It has to be his decision. It's not mine," he insisted. "I would never drink somebody's blood if he didn't want me to, even if it meant I went the rest of my life without ever drinking the blood of another person. To me drinking someone's blood without them wanting me to would be like drinking milk. I would get nothing from that blood. Just nothing. I feel as though I have a fear inside of me that if I did, I would not get what I get now. It would be very bad. If they're willing to inflict pain upon themselves, then that shows me. That's one way that I know."

It seems that it's not the blood that's important, then, since he drinks so little of it anyway. It's the willingness of another person to inflict pain on himself, to make a symbolic self-sacrifice. If someone does that, then Jack knows he's valued, even loved. The blood itself gives him nothing, not nutrition, not a change in brain chemicals, nothing, doctors say, since it isn't absorbed by the body once it gets down into the stomach. Even if he happened to drink the blood of someone who had done a lot of cocaine or drunk a lot of alcohol, he'd have to drink so much to get any kind of buzz that the blood itself would just make him sick.

It doesn't have that much to do with sex for Jack, either. When Jack first arrived for our interview, he was eager to talk about Andrew, our mutual friend and

Jack's lover. Andrew, it seems, in the kind of spirit of research that I certainly couldn't drum up, had given Jack some of his blood the previous night. But Jack was troubled about the experience.

"Andrew slit his tit last night. I drank it. I knew it was something he'd always wanted me to do. I haven't drank any blood for probably four months. I wasn't interested in the sexual part of it at all," Jack said, and Andrew confirmed this. "I mean, that's how it all began. We were in bed and whatnot. I love the physical taste of blood, the warmth, the feeling. Blood has a taste to me that nothing else compares with. I think it's the best taste in the world. There's nothing that compares to it. It's the warmth. The warmth is what really intrigues me. If it was cold, I don't know if I'd want it.

"When I drank it, I could really feel Andrew. I have a hard time understanding him and that's one of the reasons I wanted his blood. I don't understand him any more now, though, because he is really peculiar. He's complex. There are so many sides to him that I can't begin to understand him. He's one of the few people I've ever met who is that complex. Maybe everyone is that complex, but aren't willing to show it."

Jack continued, "I am a very good sleeper. I sleep ten or twelve hours easily and yesterday I had a long day. I worked all day and then I took the bus to Boston to meet Andrew. We went out to dinner with you last night and we didn't get to bed until very late. Usually, when I drink blood, I can fall asleep very easily. I'm comforted. But after drinking his blood last night, I had the most restless night of sleep. I couldn't get to sleep until after three or four in the morning and even though I never have headaches, I had the most tremendous headache. I couldn't think and it almost felt as though I was stoned. I was dazed. I could think more clearly, but I couldn't understand what I was thinking about."

Later I inspected the cut, which Andrew made beneath his nipple with a sharp X-Acto knife. It was tiny and Andrew said it didn't hurt at all. "So what was it like, being a donor?" I asked him.

"It was hot, very hot," Andrew replied enthusiastically. "Jack went nuts, groaning and hanging on to me, but it wasn't sexual. He didn't even have an erection."

In the area of rural New England where he's from, Jack has a few friends whose blood he drinks frequently. They're all straight men, and until recently none knew Jack is gay. Two are vampires themselves and Jack allows them to drink his blood. Another is simply a donor, having no desire for the hot, metallic-tasting liquid himself. Jack says they're very close and uses the word "communion" to describe their exchanges of blood, although he says he means it more in terms of community than the symbolic blood drinking done in church.

Jack insists that he drinks people's blood to get to know and understand them better. So he doesn't drink just anybody's blood—anybody who would offer. It's got to be somebody he knows well enough, and whom he's interested enough in getting to know better.

Jack knows a man who works in a hospital, taking blood samples for the lab. He goes from bed to bed, taking tubes of blood from oblivious patients, including one extra from each, which he smuggles out of work for one of his vampire friends, who is apparently unconcerned about drinking the blood of people sick enough to be in the hospital. Hematologists say that the chances of contracting any kind of illness, including AIDS, from drinking tainted blood are practically nil, since the stomach acid completely destroys these viruses. A small nick in one's mouth or gums that tends to bleed, however, does give the blood direct access to the drinker's bloodstream. It is possible to become infected that way, although, doctors insist, not likely.

Still, Jack questions the motives of some of the vampires or would-be vampires he knows, which he finds impure. He calls them "false vampires," who do it for bizarre reasons, not like his honorable one, an instinctual way of getting to know people better. He's troubled by one man in particular, who doesn't seem to be in tune with himself and seems to be doing it so that he can tell people (obviously not everybody) just to shock them.

Jack doesn't like his meat well cooked, and there are days when he feels he could eat it raw. Yet, the night before our interview, he ordered his steak tips medium. Basically, though, animal blood isn't that interesting to him. It's not alive and he says it's hard to get something from something when it's dead, because its spirit is gone. The spirit isn't within the blood anymore. You can still get something from it, he thinks, but nothing in comparison to that of a live person or an animal.

He did drink blood from a goat once. One of his donors lives on a farm and periodically the blood of the farm animals is tested, apparently for disease. While visiting, Jack drank a vial of goat blood, taken from the animal perhaps an hour earlier.

"I know that there is something spiritual in each animal's blood," he said. "But the feeling that I got was very different from what I got from Andrew. It was a very simple feeling from the goat. It was very simple, but I felt as though I understood his simplicity."

Jack's insistence that being a vampire is "heaven" is underlined by his belief that "I feel as though I have knowledge due to what I am. I know I have a knowledge. And I don't want to come across as conceited, because in no way am I any better than any living creature on this earth. But I know I have a knowledge.

"I don't feel as though I'm a complex person," he went on to say. "I am from a small town with traditional family values. People would look at me and say, 'He's the typical American boy.' I feel as though I have grown hundreds of years in mentality in some areas. I am by no means a genius. Math and calculus are not my thing. But I can look at you and look in your eyes, and I feel as though I understand you. There is, I want to say, a connection, but I don't know how to word it. I can feel you out. I can just feel it. It's something that is so normal for me to able to look at people and, in some respects, understand their thoughts."

Jack feels that his natural superiority as a vampire gives him even greater abilities. He told me he has frequent ESP experiences with the people who are close to him—his mother; Connie, the girl he lives with; and Andrew. He gave an example.

"One night Connie came home and simply looked at me and, before she said anything, I told her, 'That would be an absolutely great idea.' And she looked at me and I could see that she knew I knew. And she said, 'What?' And I said, 'Well, the Bon Jovi concert.'

"That kind of thing happens every day, and it's not just because I know her so well. Not too long ago, she went to a fairground with another man. She lied to me about where she was going. I was sitting in front of the lake eating my lunch, after I'd been working for one of my uncles, and I saw her on the skydiver. He was turning her and she got very dizzy. And when she came upright, she thought she saw me standing on the ground looking up. That night when I told her about it, she interrupted me and finished the story. Throughout that whole day, I knew. Right now, I know she's talking to her mother, and she just got done telling her brother something about his blue eyes."

He was so sincere, almost wide-eyed as he told me these tales that I didn't think for a minute that he was trying to put me on. He believed what he was saying.

"It's just something that I have. I can't predict earthquakes. I can't foresee the future. But I know what's going on in the world around me at this moment. What happened an hour ago, I could feel that an hour ago. I can have very good ideas of what will happen an hour beforehand."

When he drinks someone's blood, he believes this ESP power is intensified. He can, for a couple of days afterwards, pick up on the person, on what he's doing. And, he adds, "I think they can, in a way, pick up on what I'm doing but they don't understand it. They don't understand what they're thinking about. I know people better because I'm a vampire. It was something I was born with. The things I do I do out of instinct, and because it is instinct, my natural instinct, I naturally enjoy it."

Still, he admitted, "There are days when I'm feeling very typical, very American, and I ask myself, 'Gee, why do you do this?' When I'm in that kind of mood, I start thinking about who I really am and what I really am, and I can really scare myself. I'm still learning."

Remarks like that, about all the learning he's doing, and the fact that he was only twenty, made me wonder if he wasn't under the influence of someone else, not necessarily some evil master vampire off in the woods, but perhaps an older fellow vampire, someone who has read widely in the occult. His belief system seemed too pat, too certain for someone so young and with such peculiar habits, especially since everything else seemed so uncertain and confusing to him. He seemed easily influenced, and told me I was in the top ten of people close to him after only one dinner and an interview (even though I did come highly recommended).

Jack's life took some very dramatic turns in the next few months and I saw him only one more time. He and Andrew picked up Perry in a bar and brought him home to shave his chest. The following weekend, Jack was visiting Perry for the weekend, Andrew was having a fit, and Jack was calling me asking why Andrew was so upset. An ex-lover of Jack's blew the whistle on his homosexuality and every single member of his family refuses to speak to him now. He moved in with Perry, after having treated the two-inch cut in his groin that he got when Connie, upset by the news that Jack was bisexual, tried to cut his testicles off.

He never told Perry about his blood drinking. He

knew that Perry would not be able to handle it, much less casually slash himself with an X-Acto knife. Lately, he's started calling Andrew again, since Perry shows signs of straying.

For now, Jack searches for people, trying to find the ones that he can "feel this feeling with. I don't turn into a bat and search for them," he added, quite indignantly.

"It's a search, almost like someone would search for a lover, I guess. I'm not afraid I'll approach the wrong person. I know it when I see someone. When I'm united with these people, it is a love. We become a part of each other," he added.

As with most of us, Jack's reasons for doing what he does are mainly subconscious. Ultimately, it may have mostly to do with what he didn't get and still isn't getting from people, love and tenderness and understanding. He believes that he connects with people on a deeper, more profound level because of this special gift and he finds this connection more pleasurable than orgasm. He may be kidding himself, but he needs to see it that way.

All the vampires I've talked to have developed a strong rationale for their activities. Some have more self-knowledge than others. Some are smarter than others. Some are crazy, possibly ambulatory schizophrenics. Most are completely sane. None plan to stop drinking blood.

CHAPTER 2

I'll be glad when this is over. It's a bad script.

—Tom

October 21, 1989, John F. Kennedy Airport, Pan American Airlines, Gate 7: As I sat in the departure lounge for Budapest, I was wishing that Bram Stoker had based his Dracula character on someone else, someone in Africa or Thailand, perhaps. John Joslyn, the producer of the infamous Al Capone/Geraldo Rivera TV special "Sorry, Folks, There's Nothing in the Safe but Some Dust," was flying some 120 people to Hungary to do a live two-hour special via satellite on Dracula and vampires. Vampires are hot, hot, hot, and Joslyn was ready to jump on the bloody bandwagon. In exchange for some consulting, he had invited me along. Ten days before air time, he still didn't have a real-life vampire to appear in shadow and tell what it's really like to drink blood. And he'd been unable to contact Sean Manchester, the notorious self-proclaimed vampire hunter and killer.

Norine Dresser, author of *American Vampires* and the only consultant listed in the credits, hadn't been able to come up with a vampire for him. I immediately called Misty, who had done talk shows before. She expressed some interest, but when Joslyn called her, it turned out that she was afraid to fly over water. Later, Misty explained to me that she'd had this fear ever since she'd seen *Jaws*. The idea of being in a plane crash in the ocean and having a shark bite off her legs was too much for her. Joslyn was able, finally, to find another vampire.

Joslyn was relying on Bernard Davies of the Dracula Society in London to help him locate Sean Manchester. I knew this wouldn't work; the Dracula Society is a dignified, sophisticated group of people who are passionately interested in vampire books and films, and equally interested in not being associated in any way with Sean Manchester. Manchester claims to believe in supernatural vampires, the red-eyed, snarling type who sleep in coffins and bite the necks of girls with big breasts. He has even tramped about in cemeteries opening a tomb or two, or so he says, and staking the corpse within.

Although I did manage to contact Manchester, he didn't get word until the day before the special and, as he later told me in a letter, "Mine is a very old family, one branch of which can be traced back to the conquest and I prefer to travel by means other than an aeroplane which is why Budapest—only made known to me the day before broadcast—was ruled out."

Obviously, Joslyn had not done his research, even though the special had been in production for eleven months and, according to one member of the production staff, cost around $2 million. No doubt people were simply refusing to introduce him to or even tell him about other people in this small circle of so-called vampire experts.

The special was being filmed (and parts of it broadcast live) from Solomon's Tower in Višegrad, about an hour from Budapest. It was here that Vlad Tepes, a very nasty Rumanian prince best known as Vlad the Impaler, was imprisoned for twelve years. Born in 1431, he's considered a hero in Rumania and even appears on their postage stamps from time to time, since, when the Turks were attempting to conquer Rumania, Vlad successfully turned them back.

He was a bloodthirsty, evil man whose favorite method of execution was impalement. According to Drs. Raymond McNally and Radu Florescu, authors of several books on Vlad Tepes, Vlad killed between 40,000 and 100,000 victims during his lifetime. The sight of a forest of 24,300 victims impaled on sharp wooden stakes—some hanging half-dead in agony, others dead and decaying for weeks—scared the Turks so badly that they gave up all interest in making Rumania a suburb. Vlad was also known as Dracula, and most serious scholars believe it was this monstrous historical figure who inspired Stoker's vampire.

Florescu and McNally were on the special, too. Professors of history at Boston College, they're genuine scholars, two of the few researchers in the vampire subculture who can be taken seriously. Florescu is a descendant of Vlad's brother and was born in Rumania, where the two professors have spent most of their careers tracking down and translating old documents, and conducting expeditions to Transylvania where, among other things, they located the ruins of Vlad's castle.

John Joslyn wanted to broadcast from the ruins of Vlad's castle and tried to arrange it, but the government wouldn't let him near the ruins, offering instead a different, picturesque castle in another part of Rumania that had nothing to do with Vlad.

It's not surprising that bloody Vlad was considered a hero in Ceausescu's Rumania, one of the most repressive regimes in modern history. A bizarre AIDS epidemic among babies was one Ceausescu legacy. In Rumania, women were strongly pressured to have babies whether they wanted to or not. Ceausescu wanted workers for his country, and he also sold off the excess babies, given up to orphanages by desperate mothers who could not feed them, to a lucrative adoption market outside of Rumania.

Many of these babies developed AIDS as the result of an obsolete medical procedure, once common but now used nowhere else in the world. Quite simply, the umbilical cord of the newborn was injected with a small quantity of adult blood, intended as a sort of tonic. Since such a small amount of blood was used, it was possible to infect several hundred babies from just one tainted source.

The Rumanian government didn't want an American film crew in the highly controversial area around Vlad's castle, the region where the revolution actually began a few months later. So Joslyn opted for Hungary, bravely continuing to call it Transylvania. This fudging of the facts brought publicist Ashley Anderson quite a bit of grief as she bravely went from news office to news office in Budapest with her press kits, hoping to get some more promotion for the show.

"But this isn't Transylvania," the correspondents would tell her, and she'd have to explain about Tepes's imprisonment in Solomon's Tower.

Joslyn couldn't get Geraldo Rivera this time because Geraldo was under contract with ABC, so he recruited George Hamilton instead. Hamilton was chosen because he had played Dracula in *Love at First Bite,* which a lot of people find very funny. George turned out to be one of the pleasant surprises on this trip, at least when it came to professionalism and grace under pressure.

So I went to watch this amazing phenomenon, a two-hour special about vampires being pulled together and beamed via satellite to the homes of supposedly transfixed Americans. They'd been titillated for weeks by come-ons on Fox Television. In the commercial for the special, a pale, white hand slowly reached out of a coffin. "Live from Transylvania!" an insinuating, cruel-sounding voice said, matched by dripping red letters on the screen.

After an extremely bumpy shuttle ride from Boston, I had just settled in to wait for boarding when George Hamilton walked up to the man seated across from me and started to chat with him. I eavesdropped. It's my job. George told the man, who I later found out was named Tom and who was in charge of cue cards, that he'd been given a script which he didn't have the time to learn. George wanted cue cards—big ones. He said he couldn't read cue cards as easily as he used to. Hamilton was insistently tan, even though it's unfashionable now. A California boy, he found the late October New York weather too much for him, and he was all bundled up in a down jacket.

He finished his conversation with Tom, and I

quickly walked up to him and introduced myself. George was very friendly and introduced me to his personal assistant and to Ashley. A little boy asked for his autograph, which he absentmindedly gave.

We were then joined by Brad, the donor in the special, who gave George an account of how his fingers were stabbed with a needle and then sucked by a vampire. Brad found it sexy, the sharp, quick stab and then the slow, hard sucking on each finger. For this, he was supposed to get a thousand dollars and a trip to Budapest.

George was very curious about my research. He knew a lot about the Highgate Cemetery hoax that had first brought Sean Manchester into the public eye. Later, Ashley told me that George had gone on a tour of Highgate Cemetery, where vampires were said to have wandered in the early seventies. The tour guide, not recognizing Hamilton following along at the back of the group, was talking about how the Friends of Highgate Cemetery allow movies to be made in the cemetery for a fee, as a way of raising funds to continue renovation.

The guide then proceeded to offer his opinion of a few vampire movies, including *Love at First Bite*. The guide did not care for it, nor, he added very loudly, did he care for George Hamilton. George was understandably embarrassed, but, fortunately, remained unrecognized.

From Hamilton's bio, straight from the *Dracula—Live from Transylvania* press kit: "By now, the HAMILTON style has become a whole reality. Magazines all over the world publish features about his work, his pleasures, his customs and his loves. Serious about his work, HAMILTON says he 'acts on instinct—but, the director is the man I really study.'

"Interested in sports, he's an expert swimmer, rider, and skier, good living is important to him. In 1988, he launched the George Hamilton Skin Care System which has been hugely successful and in June of this year the George Hamilton Sun Care System was made exclusively available in Neiman-Marcus stores around the country.

"GEORGE HAMILTON is one of the few contemporary actors on the screen, combining all the 'Old Hollywood' magic that is so rare today."

George told me that he'd be glad to talk to me during the flight about what it's like to play a vampire, but when I finally made it up to first class after being fed a vile salt-and-fat entree in coach, George had nodded off.

I didn't see him again until we were all settled in the first-class lounge at the Budapest airport for what turned out to be a two-hour wait while we were given express treatment at customs. George doesn't seem to enjoy silence and constantly moved around the room, asking questions, chatting, starting conversations. At one point, he started talking about when his ex-wife Alana left him for Rod Stewart.

"We were cohosting this talk show at the time and she'd turn up half an hour late," he said. "Half an hour. I couldn't believe it. In this big limo, with Rod Stewart's name plasterd on the side. 'Alana,' I would say, 'you're half an hour late. What's the big idea?' She'd tell me that Rod was rock-and-roll and she had to stay up late. Rock and roll. You can have it."

Finally, we made our way into Budapest in assorted vans. Brad was thrilled with the old city, and eagerly snapped photos with his Instamatic through the dirty windows of the van. "Look at that beautiful mosque," he cried out, as we passed by a large, ornate church. Maybe he thought we were in Istanbul.

Tom was upset because the airline had lost his box of supplies needed to make the cue cards. He mistakenly assumed that he wouldn't be able to get ink and other such items in Budapest. He wasn't that happy to be there. "I'll be glad when this is over," he told me. "It's a bad script."

The whole production team seemed to have the impression that Budapest is still in the Middle Ages. I was warned to bring all the paper goods I needed, but my room in the Intercontinental was well stocked, with colored cotton balls, bottles of shampoo and bubble bath, and sewing kits. The average American could find almost anything he or she wanted in Budapest, from a Fender bass to Charlie perfume to McDonald's hamburgers.

The next morning, I met the show's vampire expert, Norine Dresser. She and her sweetheart of a husband, Harold, were breakfasting with Bernard Davies. Together Dresser, Davies, and Hamilton, all of whom dominated the first half-hour of the special, caused millions of viewers to it turn off, out of sheer boredom. "Here, George," Davies said during the show. "This is a typewriter very much like the one Bram Stoker used," pointing to an antique typewriter next to him. Thousands of Americans must have reached for their remote controls when Davies did that.

Dresser is well into her fifties. She has frizzy black hair and wore heavy black glasses, bright red lipstick, and nondescript clothing. She speaks loudly and authoritatively in a rather nasal voice. Dresser told me a little about Monique, the vampire that Joslyn had finally found in Boston.

"She's a real victim," Dresser said. "She got roped into some kind of a cult when she was young. It's really tragic."

"I tried to arrange for Misty to appear," I told Norine. "You know of her, I believe."

"Misty doesn't deserve to come," Dresser said sharply. "She's an awful girl."

Dresser devoted a good third of her book to a theory advanced by David Dolphin, Ph.D., a professor of chemistry at the University of British Columbia. In a paper he gave at an American Association for the Advancement of Science conference in 1985, Dolphin suggested that the extensive folklore about vampires had originated in fact, as folklore often does. Specifically, he suggested that people who drank blood, in the process inspiring vampire mythology, might be victims of porphyria.

Porphyria is an incurable genetic disease that affects around fifty thousand people in the United States. Symptoms include receding gums, which can give the appearance of fangs, and sensitivity to sunlight in varying degrees, in some cases so much that burns result in severe scarring. People with porphyria suffer from a deficiency of the enzyme that helps to synthesize heme, which is a component of hemoglobin. Dolphin suggested that perhaps, before the disease was understood, people with porphyria drank blood in an instinctual attempt to treat themselves.

Of course, the press loved Dr. Dolphin. Dresser tells in her book of the headlines that appeared at the time. In the *Washington Post:* DRACULA WOLF MAN LEGENDS

MAY CONTAIN A DROP OF TRUTH: GENETIC DISORDER MAY TRIGGER THIRST FOR BLOOD. In *Newsweek:* VAMPIRE DIAGNOSIS: REAL SICK. Even the children's publication the *Weekly Reader* wrote about Dolphin's theory, with the headline DID DISEASE TRIGGER VAMPIRES' BLOOD THIRST?

It was a great story. And Dolphin's theory, although containing some errors (porphyria victims can eat all the garlic they want, for example), makes a lot of sense. For Dresser, though, it seems to have become a cause after she learned that porphyria victims had been embarrassed, humiliated, and angered by the stories.

She brought up the porphyria controversy over the eggs and orange juice. "Nobody believes Dolphin's theory," she stated adamantly, as she states most things. "Nobody!"

I called the publicist and told her I wanted to go to the set to observe some of the shooting, and we made plans for the following evening. Ashley was having a lot of trouble getting PR for the show. Not only did the anniversary of the failed Hungarian revolution take place during the filming, but the following day was the one on which Hungary officially became a democracy. A "Super Event," no matter how well hyped, just can't compete with that.

The next day I walked down to the square in front of Parliament to witness the official ceremonies of Hungary becoming a democracy. TV cameras sat on top of cranes, and a gang of reporters and photographers waited, a few photographers doing what I was doing, wandering about, gathering impressions, taking photos. Even MTV-Europe was there, briefly blasting out Peter Gabriel's "Big Time" over the otherwise silent, immense speaker system.

The crowd built slowly, some people arriving alone, others in marching, singing groups. Many were wearing red-, white-, and green-striped armbands with OKT 23 printed on them in black, while others carried small paper Hungarian flags with holes in the centers, where the hated Soviet star had been cut out. Still others carried unlit white candles stuck through paper plates to catch the dripping wax. A woman hawked ham sandwiches from a basket over her arm. People walked their dachshunds and cocker spaniels, while kids skateboarded and bicycled. Men with brooms and dustpans, wearing fluorescent vests, immediately swept up anything that was dropped.

An old man with a deeply wrinkled face, carrying a clipping stapled to a stick, seemed shell-shocked. He remembered when the tanks had come, and was there to tell the story. He walked around blessing people, making crosses in the air, and I wondered if he was a former priest. Not an easy country to be a priest in, Hungary didn't even allow priests to visit people in the hospital until four months before our trip, someone later told me. Now all that is changed, and I stopped into several churches while walking in Budapest, where people kneeled and prayed openly and priests swung censers of incense at them. Everybody seemed to be so relieved that at last they could go to church.

A large Hungarian flag on a tall flagpole off to one side of the square was guarded by an honor guard of five soldiers, who had small Hungarian flags hanging ridiculously from their bayonets. As the crowd gathered, another soldier came from inside the Parliament building. He shouted orders, and the soldiers left the flag, goose-stepping into the distance, as quiet applause filled the square. And then, one by one, the people took over, stepping into the positions the soldiers had held, standing, just standing, quietly and proudly. Old women wearing babushka-style scarves held up banners proclaiming freedom. I hid behind my camera to conceal my tears.

Joslyn was doing his filming at night, since even though no more than a half hour of the special was actually to be telecast live, the idea was to give the impression that it was almost all live. When I went to meet Ashley for the hourlong drive to the set, I was introduced to Dr. Raymond McNally.

McNally is a very good-looking man, tall, with a booming voice, handsome Irish features, and a gorgeous shock of white hair. I'd talked to him when I was first getting interested in vampires and we renewed our acquaintance during the drive. He and Florescu had recently written a new book, *Dracula: Prince of Many Faces,* and I asked him what was new in the book, since they'd been writing about Vlad Tepes in different books for years. He told me about his discovery in Rumania of a letter documenting that old Vlad, yes, drank blood, specifically that he had dipped bread into a bowl of the blood of some of his victims and munched it down.

I told him that I was also writing about real-life vampires. McNally has carefully avoided the subject for years, even though he's been approached and received letters from people claiming to be vampires. There's often a dark figure at the back of the lecture hall when Florescu and McNally speak about their research, lurking, waiting for a chance to speak to the professors alone. They leave by a back door whenever possible.

"I think these people are pathetic and sick," Mc-

Nally boomed, as we zipped along in the cold Hungarian night. "I won't have anything to do with them. I don't think anyone else should be dealing with them either. It could be dangerous and these people need professional help. Not to say that you shouldn't be talking to them," he added, after saying in effect that I shouldn't be talking to them.

The set was surrounded by large trailers filled with expensive equipment. Large ropes of cables taped together ran everywhere. A huge satellite dish sat nearby in dramatic contrast to the old castle, which had been beautifully renovated by the Hungarian government and was now a regular tourist attraction. I followed Ashley to the tower where Vlad had spent twelve years in a tiny cell, and we slowly climbed the steps to the top, where George and Dr. Florescu had just finished filming. Ashley introduced me to John Joslyn and while we chatted on the steps, George came down and said, "I think we've got a problem."

For some reason, there wasn't a script supervisor on the set, and Hamilton had just shot a scene without his overcoat, which was supposed to precede a scene in which he is wearing his overcoat and, in fact, makes a bad joke about the coat. The tension in the air was palpable and the director looked very unhappy. With the show already four hours behind schedule, it seemed as though they were going to have to shoot the scene over again. Joslyn had a tense smile on his face as they discussed the alternatives, including rewriting part of the script. Hamilton, however, saved the day by suggesting that he comment at the beginning of his next scene that he was chilly, and that someone simply slip his overcoat on his shoulders, as a little joke.

Throughout the filming, which was always two hours or more behind schedule, Hamilton kept up a running rap of commentary and jokes. He helped direct the guests, who were almost all nonprofessionals. George knew he was on a sinking ship, and as Tom told me later, they laughed together about the terrible script throughout filming, while at the same time hanging in there, trying to keep everybody's spirits up and doing their jobs.

The rehearsal for the next scene went on and on and on. At the end of the scene, during which Dr. Florescu provided some more information about Vlad, he was supposed to invite Hamilton to dinner. He had said the line wrong, though, instead inviting Hamilton "for" dinner, and Hamilton thought this was funny, so Florescu had to get used to saying the line that way.

The live broadcast, which aired at eight P.M. on the East Coast, actually took place at one in the morning in Hungary. A van took Monique the vampire, Brad the donor, Dresser, her husband Harold, Ashley Anderson, and me out to the set to watch. Dresser spoke warmly of Hamilton, and recounted how he had made her so comfortable by taking her aside to go over their scene together.

Monique, the token vampire, was mad at Hamilton, because even though he kept eyeing her from a distance, he refused to interview her on camera. Hamilton just didn't think interviewing vampires and their donors was in keeping with his image. That function, unfortunately, fell to Dresser.

Monique is an attractive woman in her mid-twenties. She was unhappy with her time in Budapest. She'd come down with a cold and was mad because nobody had cared enough to see how she was doing and maybe get her some cough medicine. Except for some time spent with Brad, who offered to donate some blood on the spot (an offer which she declined), she'd been on her own.

She became angry when I told her that I'd heard she was the victim of a drug cult.

"Victim! What a narrow-minded view of experience! I wasn't a victim," she said indignantly. Monique told me she had entered an ashram where she had stayed for about four months, meditating, fasting periodically, eating a vegetarian diet when she wasn't fasting, forgoing sex, alcohol, and drugs, and speaking very little.

"At the end of the four months," Monique said, "I went to see a friend, held out my arm, and he shot me up with a dose of heroin. My arm was bleeding from the needle. So my friend bent down and licked it up. Then he filled the syringe with my blood and squirted it into his mouth. And that's how it all started."

For three years, she and several other people would meet and drink blood from time to time. Monique is an artist and lives with a boyfriend, although at the time she was in Budapest she was having an affair with another man.

"He's a criminal," she told me. "He steals things every so often. He'll just make a whole truckload of something disappear. I think that's very sexy."

We all settled in to watch the show on a monitor. "Trick or treat, I'm in my George Hamilton costume. Come and check it out," Hamilton joked as he pounded on the door of the castle. Hamilton then spent the rest of the special running around the castle, pretending to be scared, while various experts would pop up behind doors.

His first interview was with Radu Florescu. Florescu dragged his lines, speaking much too slowly to hold the viewer's interest. Then came a scene with Norine Dresser at home, typing on her computer. Dresser looked awful, in part because she was lit in an extremely unflattering way. "The vampire is almost a classic Halloween figure," she informed us. Almost?

Then Hamilton read aloud from Bram Stoker's *Dracula*. This was probably where a lot of people turned the special off. But if they stuck it out, Bernard Davies was next, and although Bernard is a very nice man and an expert on Bram Stoker, he does go on and on. At one point Davies forgot his lines, and together he and Hamilton were beamed into space staring wordlessly at the camera.

In probably the liveliest and most interesting segment of the whole show, since McNally is so articulate, he and Florescu discussed Vlad the Impaler and some of his unpleasant antics. McNally also discussed porphyria, connecting it with vampirism. Norine Dresser clicked her tongue in anger as she watched the monitor.

Later in the show a body was found "without a drop of blood in it," and Hamilton was running around the castle with a stake, mallet, and torch, jumping at the sound of a howling wolf, followed by a fictional Radu character, who was eventually done in by a vampire, too. Finally, the narrator's voice promised, "When we return, we'll meet real-life vampires, who might just be your next-door neighbor."

When the show resumed Dresser told Hamilton, who wasn't pretending to be aghast this time, "Yes, they even drink blood. I found in my research that vampires can be flight attendants, hospital workers, you never know.

"After eighteen months, I made a very strange discovery," Dresser said as a lead-in to a re-creation of an act of vampirism, during which an actress pretended to poke Brad's fingers with an enormous needle and then suck blood from them. The long canines of the actress chosen to play the vampire broke up everybody watching the monitor and turned the whole thing into a joke.

"What was that?" Hamilton asked. "That was one of the weirdest things I've ever seen. You can't be serious. People do that for fun? Why?"

"There are people on the other side of that door who can answer that question for you," Dresser told him.

"Vampires?" Hamilton cried, pretending to be terrified.

"Yes," responded Dresser.

"Vampires?" Hamilton asked again. "Real vampires? And you're telling me they're here?"

"Would you like to meet them?" asked Dresser.

"No," said Hamilton. "No. Meeting real vampires wasn't in my deal."

"Well, suit yourself," Dresser replied, as she awkwardly moved toward the door, obviously terrified of having to walk somewhere on camera.

"It's one thing to talk about fifteenth-century vampires," Hamilton said, "but 1989, forget it. She does this kind of thing for a living. Just go ahead in. I'll stand guard out here." Dresser opened the door to the room where Brad and Monique waited. "Yes, sir, I'll just wait out here. What about you?" he asked the audience. "OK. You're gonna be sorry."

Dresser walked up to two people standing in shadow.

"Hi, Brad," she said, greeting him with inappropriate brightness. "It's good to see you. You've told me you're a donor. Does that mean you give blood to vampires?"

"I did," Brad replied.

"Well," asked Dresser, "can you tell me how that came about?"

"Well," answered Brad, plunging into his narrative eagerly, "I met a woman who, in all other respects, seemed to be functioning, married, had a full-time job. I myself had an interest in horror movies and this woman professed a desire to drink blood. And I decided to experiment on a personal level to further acquaint myself with this."

"Mmm-hmm," replied Dresser. "And tell me, what does the drinking of blood do for you? In other words, why? I can understand your being curious about it, you know, but why are you really doing it beyond the curiosity?"

"The reason that I did it principally was because I was amazed that a person could drink blood altogether on a scientific level," Brad attempted to explain. "I did find that it gave me a pleasurable feeling after the act was performed. It was a pleasurable feeling, more like wanting to fall asleep after a hard day on the job, so to speak."

Uh-uh. Brad's not telling the truth here. It could be because he's been told not to, but the real reason he did it was because it turned him on.

We sat through the taped sections of the show twice, first on a test transmission, and then again when the show was broadcast live, with the added taped sections, which made up the vast majority of the show. Both times, as the section with Monique approached, she got up and left the room. She didn't want to see it. The second time Monique got up to leave, Dresser called her a coward.

"And Monique, it's nice to have you here," Dresser began. "Do you consider yourself a vampire?"

"Yes, I do," replied Monique.

"And that means that you actually drink human blood?" Dresser asked.

"Yes," replied Monique.

"How long has this been going on?" Dresser demanded, the way a parent would confront a teenager caught with a joint in her jewelry box.

"About six years," said Monique.

"Six years," repeated Dresser. "I see. And about how often does this occur?"

"Well, it goes in cycles. Sometimes it can be consecutively for three or four days, sometimes a couple of weeks, or sometimes every couple of months."

"You consume blood, what are we talking, in what kinds of quantities?" Dresser asked, making a little glass-raising motion with her hand. For some reason, Monique told me later, this question really pissed her off.

"Well, I never measured it," Monique replied.

Dresser laughed. "Gallon? Quart? Teaspoon?" she pressed.

"I'd say about half a glass," Monique finally ventured.

"Oh, that much," Dresser said, seemingly shocked at this amount, which is actually quite typical of the amount all the vampires I've ever talked to say they drink.

"And it's easy for your donors to give forth that much at one time, or you would you say that's cumulative in one setting or one feeding or whatever you want to call it?"

"Ah, at one time," Monique told her.

"One time, from one person. I see," Dresser said. What does she see?

"And from what part of the body," Dresser continued with her fascinating questions, "do you take the blood?"

The fireplace flickered gently behind Monique's shadow as she answered, "From a vein or an artery."

"So we're talking from the arm," Norine concluded.

"Mmm-hmm," Monique replied.

"Thank you both very much," Dresser said.

Cut to George. "Those two should really hit it off well," he commented. "You don't even have to make dinner reservations. All you have to do is have a quick bite and make sure there's a Band-Aid."

He rounded the corner and bumped into Bernard Davies again. "Oh, thank goodness, Bernard, I'm so glad it's you," George whimpered, pretending badly to be scared. "I just came from the dungeon and you wouldn't believe what I saw."

"George, you look ghastly," Bernard observed.

"I look ghastly!" George exclaimed, and he really did exclaim it. "You should see them. I was with Norine Dresser and there were live 1989 vampires and they were talking about bloodletting and drinking and donors, and it's sick, it's sick!"

Joslyn wasn't concerned about the feelings of his guests, that's for sure. Neither was the director, whose comments we could hear as we watched the monitor, and who voiced pretty much the same sentiments: "Who are these people? They're sick." Since Monique had already left, she didn't hear this, but Brad did and seemed quite hurt. He considered himself adventurous and daring, not sick.

It was now four in the morning, and as I stepped outside John Joslyn walked by. "Great show," I said insincerely, as I shook his hand.

"Come on over to the buffet we're having," he invited me. I wandered over and started talking to Monique, who was seething quietly.

"They took a lot of what I said on an interview tape, that vampires might even be your next-door neighbor, and put it into Norine's mouth," she complained. "But I signed the tape over to them, so I guess they could do what they want with it."

Dresser, who had declared herself a vegetarian earlier in the week, eagerly helped herself to the spicy meatballs on the buffet. She bounced up to John Joslyn and said, "I do other things besides vampires, you know."

John Joslyn managed to smile as we checked out of the Intercontinental the next day, even after he knew that he'd followed his record of the first and second highest-rated TV specials—Geraldo opening Capone's safe and another live from the Titanic—with a bomb. The special flopped dismally, costing Joslyn half a million dollars, according to a member of the production staff.

Monique said she would call me after she returned from Munich, but I didn't hear from her for nearly three months. She told me that she'd avoided calling because she'd been so disillusioned with the special. She'd had an abortion in that time, pregnant by the

VCR-stealing boyfriend, who had not been doing very well, since his phone had been disconnected and she'd had to write him a letter telling him of the pregnancy. His response was no response. That was over, she said.

She and her live-in boyfriend had been fighting a lot, and she was now looking for an inexpensive studio apartment, to get away from men for a while, be alone, maybe do some painting. She'd lost her job, but Massachusetts had the lowest bond rating of any of the fifty states at the time, so she had lots of company.

She looked great when we finally met for an interview. Another reason she had felt so awful in Budapest, it turned out, was that she had been anemic, which she discovered at the same time as her pregnancy. Now medically in good shape, Monique seemed relaxed and ready to talk. She lit a cigarette, and started telling her story.

Monique hated her mother. When that crucial relationship goes awry, very often so does a person's life. So it was with Monique.

"She was just impossible," Monique said. "She probably was not a bad person at one time, but she had just let everything get to her so much that there was just nothing good about her. I mean, she didn't steal or do anything like that, but she was a nasty, nasty, nasty person. She was really bitter about life. She'd never trust anyone. I swore I would never be like my mother. She never said a good thing to me. I don't think she loved anybody. I don't really think she loved herself."

Monique's mother was an artist, and lived in the glorious Bohemian Greenwich Village of the 1950s, painting well enough to appear in shows. When she met Monique's father, she got married and moved to the suburbs. First she had a son, then, four years later, Monique, but by then the marriage was over. Monique was plunked into a foster home at the age of one, while her mother went back to Greenwich Village to paint. Monique was never able to learn much about her father. All her mother would say was that he was an alcoholic, which may or may not have been true. A family friend told Monique of the existence of her older brother, who went with her father at the time of the divorce, and that her father had made attempts to see his little girl, but had always been refused by her mother. Monique wants to find her father and brother, but hasn't had the money to pursue it.

The six years in the foster home were very happy, and Monique credits any good qualities she might have to her foster parents. Even though her foster mother was quite ill and Monique had to keep fairly quiet and wasn't allowed to have friends over, she felt loved in that home. Her real mother would come to visit, bringing presents and taking her to the park and the zoo, and Monique always enjoyed the visits, which were short enough to prevent any problems.

When Monique's mother remarried, she claimed Monique. Although her foster parents wanted to keep her and Monique wanted to stay with them, her mother insisted that Monique come and live in New York City, where she attended private schools. A deep enmity began to develop between mother and daughter. Although Monique's stepfather was a "sweetheart," he was unable to protect Monique from her mother.

"She was a real tyrant," Monique continued. "Nothing was ever perfect enough for her. And I was the epitome of everything she did not like. She wanted me to be something I wasn't and she would not look at me and see me for what I was. She wanted me to be intelligent. She wanted me to be a professional. She wanted me to marry the right person. She wanted me to do all this, and it wasn't me. She never listened to me about what I wanted. I won dozens of ribbons for equestrian jumping and also won a number of swimming meets. Even when I did well in school, she would say, 'Well, this isn't good enough.' "

When Monique was ten, she was with her mother at their house in Florida. Monique had just been swimming and was wearing a swimming suit and a pair of flip-flops, carrying a towel over her shoulder, when her mother blew up at her. Monique doesn't even remember why.

"Why don't you just leave?" her mother screamed at her. "I don't want you here."

So Monique did. The skinny little ten-year-old girl marched up the highway in her flip-flops and bathing suit, not looking back. She eventually found a hotel where a lot of children were swimming and playing on a water slide and she just joined in. She stayed there for three days, sleeping on the pool lounges, using hotel towels for blankets. All she had to eat in that time was a candy bar and a soda. Not once did the little girl ask an adult to call her mommy. Finally, the police found her and took her home to the welcoming arms of her mother. They were welcoming only while the police were still there. After they left, the grinding psychological abuse started again.

Her stepfather, Monique's one buffer against her mother, died when she was eleven. Eight months later, Monique made a serious suicide attempt, taking some of her mother's sleeping pills. The family psychiatrist chalked the attempt up to despondency over her stepfather's death and nothing was done to discover the true cause of a child's desperate act. Finally, just to get away from her mother, Monique asked to go to boarding school and, at the age of thirteen, she was sent to a Catholic school. She didn't last long there. The school, which opened students' mail, learned that Monique had smoked pot and she was out after just a few months.

Several more boarding schools followed. When Monique was fifteen, her mother committed suicide. The only available relatives were her stepfather's parents and Monique wanted no part of that, becoming instead an emancipated minor. She returned to upstate New York, where the headmaster of an alternative high school allowed her to earn her high-school diploma, while giving her the time she needed to work to pay for her room in a rooming house. Monique's first job was as a janitor, a far cry from the private schools, riding lessons, and trips abroad that had been characteristic of her life until her mother's death.

Monique had been cut out of her mother's will. Her maternal uncle and his wife had had a Down syndrome child. Monique, herself constantly criticized and harassed, had watched in astonishment as her mother fell in love with the baby, doting on it, and eventually she left her sizable estate to the child. Monique didn't care about the money for a long time. She was free. When she was twenty, after a couple of years at a community college, Monique moved to Boston.

"I was searching," she said. "I was into rock and roll and art, and I was also interested in Eastern religion. So I went into an ashram for four months. It wasn't a cult. We weren't told not to associate with people from the outside or asked to give up all our money and possessions. They didn't just grab people in off the street like the Hare Krishnas. I could leave any time I wanted to. It was a religious community working toward enlightenment. I stayed for four months, eating a vegetarian diet, meditating, and speaking very little.

"I was working in a restaurant and I met some people there who had a lot of the same interests and tastes I did. One night, after all this clean living for four months, I decided I wanted to get high. So I went with these people over to their house. I was looking for heroin. I'd never shot it, but I had smoked it and I liked that high.

"A guy named Jim set it up for me. He put the needle in my arm and injected the heroin. He moved the needle back and forth in my arm to make the blood flow. It didn't really hurt, no more than getting your ear pierced. Then, when the syringe was full, he drank the blood in it. I thought this was odd at first. But I just sat there, because I'm a very curious person. It wasn't hurting me. I wasn't scared."

So it began. Eventually, Monique and seven other people, of both sexes, met to exchange blood, sometimes doing drugs, sometimes not. Demerol was popular. The tablets were broken up and mixed with water in a fluted glass, then injected. For Monique, just the act of giving or receiving blood provided the rush. It wasn't physical energy that she felt. She described it simply as a very warm feeling.

The group was tightly knit. To Monique, it felt like a

family. Several of the members were rock musicians, another was a comic-strip artist, another a playwright and actor. Monique herself is an artist, interested especially in furniture design. Two members of the group had been in the same ashram as Monique.

"I don't really have any roots and that's a big reason I joined the group. I believe that the communion between us was a higher state of mind," Monique said. "We were all seekers. We weren't out of control. Everybody had this need to have a really strong bond. It was a spiritual activity. We all loved each other.

"I felt good. I didn't feel as though I did anything wrong. I didn't feel embarrassed or remorseful. I felt as though I opened myself up in a way that made me feel less fear, and the whole experience has left me with less fear. I'm afraid of things I should be afraid of, though, like Papa Doc."

For three years they met, sometimes every night for week after week, sometimes not for several months. Late at night or in the early, early morning, with the Sex Pistols or the Ramones playing in the background, they would casually break up into couples or groups of three and, almost always using syringes, exchange blood among themselves. Leo, the playwright, mainlined Monique's blood one day, smiling the whole time because he enjoyed it so much. He asked her to take blood from a vein in his penis, but she refused, because she thought it would hurt him. Monique takes blood only from a person's hands or arms. Sometimes it tastes like iron, but at other times it tastes very sweet or salty.

Sex wasn't important to the group, at least not with each other. Although Monique, who is bisexual, eventually had an intimate relationship with Julie, members didn't sleep together for the most part.

They gradually broke up, after two members moved to San Francisco, two others to Paris. Jim, who introduced Monique to blood drinking, goes to AA now and refuses to discuss the past, even to the point of getting an unlisted phone number. Julie is engaged to a rock musician who loathes Monique, resenting her past intimate relationship with Julie, so Monique rarely gets to see her once-close friend. All the members of the group have since had AIDS tests, all negative. Monique has had three, all negative.

Monique hasn't found anybody to share blood with in the three years since the group broke up. Now, when Monique wants it, she takes her own, and has many scars in the crook of her arm. It brings back happy memories, she says, and she feels a rush of energy from it. Late one night, while she was walking through Boston's Kenmore Square, where most of the rock clubs are located, a young man who looked like a student approached her and asked her to share blood with him. She quickly walked away, frightened, not wanting to get involved, not that way, not with a stranger. She too believes that vampires just recognize each other.

Monique has incorporated a lot of Buddhist beliefs into her world view, and respects the Buddhist religion. She has not been able to conform to it, even though she has tried. She believes that she has lived a lot of lives, as different sexes, in different time periods, and that she possibly even lived in a primitive time. She feels that all the people in her family of blood drinkers were very old souls as well and that she'd known at least some of them in previous lives, since she hit it off so well with them almost immediately.

"My mind is so strong," she said, "that I can sometimes tell what a person is feeling. I can feel things, too. I don't want to use the word *predict*. I have a sense of when things are going to happen. I think by living all these lives you acquire all this psychic energy.

"For instance, when I was a child, my stepfather was in the hospital. I didn't know exactly what was going on. I just knew that he was sick and in the hospital. But I knew the time that he died. I was at home alone and I knew that he was dead. A few minutes later, my stepuncle came in and told me that my stepfather had died. And sometimes I can help somebody look for something and, even if I don't know their apartment or anything, I'll find it. It's like I set my mind to find it."

Sensitive people often can tell what another person is feeling, and Monique is extremely sensitive. Like all of us, she needs to feel special and so attaches great importance to what she feels are psychic abilities. She clings strongly to her self-image as a creative person and an artist as another way of feeling special. Of course, most special of all, she's a vampire.

Not surprisingly for the daughter of a cold, unloving mother, Monique has had a lot of bad relationships. She admits that she's very needy; that she needs excitement, variety, and diversity, or she becomes very depressed. At the same time, she feels that she's a loner destined to be alone.

"Every once in a while, when I'm down and out, I feel as though I'm unlovable and that I'll never be able to have a good relationship. I wonder if I'm ever going to get anywhere. But I'm fortunate because I've experienced a lot and I've traveled a lot for my age. I happen to be very intelligent without a lot of schooling. I have the ability to figure things out, so that's what's really gotten me through," she said.

"I do get lonely, but a lot of the time I really feel that I need to be alone. I feel that I have to be alone because of my childhood, because of my mother. I may have inherited a little bit of her mental illness. Sometimes I'll get really emotional about things, or I will get really depressed. I spent a lot of years hating myself. My mother brought that onto me. Even though there are a lot of things I want to change about myself, basically I like myself. I do, in spite of all my faults.

"I need to create. Painting is my love. I try to do things that make me confident, and I try not to lean on other people or get too emotionally attached to people. It just has never really worked out for me. Maybe I haven't found that thing I'm supposed to do yet. But when I find it, I'm going to spend all of my energy doing it, because I'm an extremist. I don't have any balance. I need to be doing something new, something different. Otherwise, I might go totally downhill.

"I think people who drink blood should be able to go to blood banks to buy blood, blood that's safe and has been tested for AIDS. I'd buy that kind of blood, if I knew it was safe," Monique told me. "After all, that's basically what I do when I buy meat. And, when I do buy meat, I barely cook it. I like it very rare. If I could, I'd buy animal blood to drink. It should be there on the grocery store shelves for people who want it. It's probably a lot safer than human blood."

She recently began taking the antidepressant Prozac, and has vowed to stay drug-free to give the

Prozac a chance to really work. She knows that she's depressed, probably biochemically so, and wants to get well so she can get on with her life. Monique doesn't know if she will leave blood drinking behind her.

CHAPTER 3

A couple once wrote to me and told me they needed a pair of vampire's eyes so that they could rule the world. They said that if I didn't send them my eyes in two weeks, they would come and get them. Did they really think I'd be stupid enough to pluck out my eyes and send them to them? How could I see to address the box if I didn't have my eyes?

—COUNTESS MISTY

Vampires drink blood for many reasons, and the reasons they give are seldom the real reasons, which are almost always kicking around in their unconscious, for not even them to know. One of the most compelling reasons is power. Many blood drinkers are disenfranchised, powerless people with little hope for the future. To actually convince someone to injure himself or to permit you to injure him, to give you his life's blood, can feel very empowering. It may be the only power they will ever have. For people who have fallen through the cracks of society, often lacking a loving home, education or the intelligence to pursue it, and the social skills necessary to have healthy relationships, blood drinking also satisfies the need to feel special and the desire for attention.

Misty is one of these disenfranchised vampires. She has created an elaborate belief system around her blood drinking in order to romanticize and justify it, seemingly borrowing most of her beliefs from vampire movies. Misty calls her blood drinking her "need." Her family told her that as soon as she had her first tooth, she began chewing on her skin, tearing at her hands until they bled. She believes that she was born a vampire, and that she inherited it from her grandfather, who drank glasses of blood and frequently cooked with blood as well. She once asked her grandfather if he was, like her, a vampire. He said he was, and that the vampirism went back generations in their family. She admits that she doesn't know if he drank and cooked with human blood; many cultures have recipes containing animal blood.

"Whenever he would see me doing something or if I'd be walking around pacing, he'd say, 'Why don't you sit down here. I know what you need.' I got hooked on one of his dishes. It's called chocolate meat. It's pork meat that's fried up in blood," she explained. "You have to mix in vinegar and your spices and all this. You got to prepare it, and the blood is prepared in a certain way, and you have to whip it to where it turns like a foam, and then you boil, then you add your meat and fry it in there. And then you put your rice on the plate and put the sauce and the meat on top. It's real good. He used to fix that, and I used to sit there and watch him do it whenever I'd smell the blood in the house."

Misty has virtually mythologized her grandfather,

who came from the Philippines. He was always supportive of her when she came home crying that the other children were calling her a bloodsucker. He once told her, "You can't just go out and talk to anybody. They don't understand. You have to remember this. And always look over your shoulder. If you hear somebody behind you, you turn around, whether you think it's nothing or not. If it's dead silence, you turn around and look, too, because there's something going to be there."

She says people avoided her grandfather because he was a prankster. She also tells tales of him as a cutup in school, doing such things as putting red ink on a little girl's chair.

"When he was in school," Misty said, "the teacher asked him if he knew how to chase mosquitoes out of the house. He raised his hand and said, 'Yes, ma'am.' She said, 'How do you do it?' He said, 'First you get a whole bunch of blankets, you pile them up in the middle of the room, and you set them afire. That will chase them all out.' She asked, 'Well, is there another way?' He said, 'Yes, you take Karo syrup, rub it on a plate, and fling it around the house and it catches flies and mosquitoes.'

"I was raised by my grandmother and my uncle," she said, "which they are now deceased. They were like mother and father to me, and I loved them very much. When my mother was in labor with me in the hospital, my father was gone off to another state to be with his parents instead of being with my mother. So my grandmother went in with my mother when she was having me. And something was mentioned that when the baby was born that it was supposed to be put up for adoption. I was left in the hospital to be adopted. And my grandmother decided after five or six days, somewhere in there, to take me, because she wanted to keep the family together."

Misty is inconsistent about whom she lived with when she grew up, but no matter where she was, she was miserable. First she said that she lived in a hotel her grandmother managed, from the time she left the hospital until she was seventeen.

"I had no childhood," she said. "I was not allowed to see friends, only at school, only a few. But then after they went to different schools, I never saw them again. I don't know why she wouldn't allow me to see my friends. She wouldn't let me out. I couldn't go to the parks and play. I stayed at the hotel. I did maid work. I did janitorial and I was also desk clerk. She showed me how to do the hotel bookkeeping and everything, raised me up, and when I was eight years old I was doing all the maid work myself, all the janitorial. I couldn't go in any recreation things. People could not come to visit me, and I just couldn't take it no more. I wasn't hardly allowed to do anything.

"Here's the way it was. When I'd come home from school, I had to do maid and janitorial on weekdays. I'd have my supper, take my bath, and go to bed. This was every day. Saturdays and Sundays I hated, because on the weekends I had to clean the halls, do the banisters. We had a two-story hotel. There were thirty-four rooms altogether. And she used to put a time limit on me, give me so much time to do all the rooms, vacuum, change towels, empty garbage, clean the sink, dust and all. And a lot of times I got my butt spanked for not finishing in time. My uncle used to sneak up and help me do the maid work so I wouldn't get in trouble."

Of course, there are child labor laws, and it is hard to imagine an eight-year-old child doing all the maid work in a thirty-four-room hotel without eventually being noticed by the authorities, who have noticed many of Misty's activities throughout her life. Probably she did help in the hotel, but not to the degree she remembers or at such a young age. Today, she still earns extra money by doing cleaning jobs.

At the very beginning of our interviews, Misty said to me, "Now, don't go using any big words. I don't like that." She was unable during several conversations with me to figure out the difference between our time zones.

Misty's grandmother was a deeply religious Christian, and she set strict limits on the little girl. The two watched game shows together, such as *Jeopardy* and *Concentration,* which Misty said they watched for "more brain power, you know. It was good education for me at home as well as what I was learning at school." Although Misty says she loved her grandmother very much, it's not clear why. Describing their relationship, she said, "We never hardly spoke much. She was mostly either sleeping or she'd gone off to bingo, or she'd be watching her TV and eating."

It was at the hotel that she remembers seeing *Dark Shadows* for the first time. "I turned on the TV and it showed Barnabas on there where he was attacking some woman. And I said, wait a minute, what is this weird movie? It said, *Dark Shadows.* I said, I don't know. I watched it and the next day I went to watch it again and my grandmother saw something on the TV and she turned it off and said, 'That might give you bad ideas.' I was never allowed to watch horror movies and things like that."

Misty continued to chew on her hands and drink her own blood. Although she said she lived with her grandmother from birth to the age of seventeen, she also apparently lived with her parents some of the time. According to Misty, their reaction to her self-mutilation was to neglect medical intervention and to try to break her will.

"They tied me down. They tried to break me from it. They took all my stuff out from my room, anything I could play with or distract myself with, and they tied me down. They put a blanket or something over the windows where it blacked everything out. They said I'd be there like for a week. My legs were tied and my hands were tied to each side of the bed."

It doesn't fit her story of child labor in the hotel, of course. At times, she had her own bedroom at home, filled with toys. When I challenged the inconsistency, she said, "Well, they would get mad at my grandmother for any little thing and I would have to come home to them. I would last two days. I would get sick. Then they would call my grandmother back up and say, 'She's sick. You'd better come and get her.' So then she or my uncle would come and get me and take me to the doctor. I would have to get medicines and my grandmother would pay the bill. There was nothing like welfare. She supported me all on her own from what she made from the hotel work, paid for all my medications, my doctor care and all this, and made sure I would get well. This would last for a couple of weeks and then my parents would get upset and want me back home. All this through my childhood, back and forth, till I was sixteen years old. I did not have an enjoyable childhood.

"It was a lot of confusion I was going through, so at

sixteen I just got tired of it. I started drinking vodka straight because of all the stuff that was going on at home. People were mean to me. Anything I needed, make your grandmother and your uncle buy it. This is the way it was. If you need school supplies, you need clothes, you need shoes, you need this and that, your grandmother and your uncle can buy it for you. We're not buying you nothing. Everything they got for the boys, for my four brothers. They favored the boys. They did not favor me at all. When I stayed with my parents, I stayed up in my room by myself. Either I watched TV or I played my records up there."

It's easy to speculate that this troubled and sickly child must have been a great burden to her caretakers, whether her parents or her grandmother. They seemed to have no idea what to do with her, and so, perhaps in an effort to make her happy, she would be sent to stay with Grandma when things were going badly at home, which they apparently so often were. Her brothers thought she was "weird" and told their friends so.

"Everybody was afraid of me. I think a lot about what happened to me in the past, and sometimes I get depressed because of it," she said, her voice deeply weighted with self-pity.

Whatever the reason, Misty didn't get what she believed she deserved from her family. She claims that her family was wealthy. She also claims that her father told her that Vincent Price was his uncle, and it was this connection that was responsible for her behavior. Price has never responded to her letters.

She claims to have begun drinking the blood of others during childhood. In the girls' bathroom, down the hall at school, the little girls would gather to prick their fingers and allow Misty to suck their blood. She wasn't popular in class. She said, "Everybody picked on me because I was what they called the ugliest kid in the school. I was smaller. I wore glasses." By the time she was ten, the kids were calling her a vampire.

She married twice, first at eighteen, to someone she met at her grandmother's hotel, whom she later divorced. Her second marriage resulted in two children, ending also in divorce after the birth of her daughter, her second child. (Her son had been born three years earlier.) Misty is absurdly coy about both her age and her weight. After adding up the events of her life, including her marriages and ten years living with another man, she's probably in her middle to late thirties. Although in our first interview she told me she was only three to four pounds overweight, she eventually admitted that it was an extra thirty to forty pounds.

Misty's children know that she believes she's a vampire and consider it normal. She said they "don't show no traces" of being vampires themselves, which pleases her. It's a hard life, constantly becoming ill and needing to drink blood to recover. When the urge comes upon her, she describes it as feeling sick, as if she's going to pass out. "It's not a very pleasant feeling," she said.

When asked how she feels when her children fall down and come to her crying with bloody knees and elbows, she said, "I've had to push that past." Misty insists that she has never drunk the blood of any children, including her own, or, for that matter, any elderly people.

Upon meeting Misty, one immediately notices her pasty, blotchy complexion. She is anemic, and her anemia has been a chronic problem throughout her life. This blood condition, along with the childhood stories of her bloody self-abuse, further fueled by the fantastic images of vampire movies, form the basis for her belief that she is a vampire. At times, she's been so severely anemic that her life has been endangered and she's been hospitalized for blood transfusions. She didn't like getting blood that way. The needles hurt and the blood felt cold.

Although doctors have given her iron supplements, she refuses to take them, insisting that they upset her stomach. She has been offered alternative medication and carefully instructed in how to maintain a high-iron diet, but Misty behaves as if she has a vested interest in staying anemic.

She believes that she has to drink blood to stay alive. She drinks blood only a few times a week, and then only a few tablespoons, although in the past she used to drink much more. She says the blood makes her stay young.

"A lot of people have noticed this too, especially those that know me so well. They'll say, 'You look like you're about like 50, 60 years old. You haven't gone out and got your bite, did you?' I says, 'No.' And they say, 'Well, how long has it been?' I say, 'About a week; almost two.' They say, 'Well, if you need it, you need it.' When I do go like every other day, they'll say, 'You look like you were from 19 to 22, 23, no older than that.' Scientists are trying to figure out with the help of vampires that they can find out what it is in the blood element in there that causes the aging process to slow down. They're trying to find out what it is and make it available to other people who want to live a little longer. It's slowed down, the biological clock, they are slowed down. It's true," she told me.

Misty prefers getting her blood "fresh," straight from the donor. She likes to bite people. "The person that's giving feels closer to me, this is what they tell me," she said. Closeness is something Misty craves.

Shortly after our first interview, Misty sent me eleven typed red pages with information that she thought would help me better understand her. The red pages are written in the third person; in them Misty describes herself as she wants to be seen.

She doesn't understand when people say they are Vampires & they drink blood as a ritual thing. BLOOD is a need, not a ritual. This need is a physical need, not a psychological need or an ego trip. "I've never heard of anyone getting high on blood unless they added a drug to it," Misty quotes herself. "Many people say the need is a fetist type thing, but I can truthfully say it is not!"

Afraid that she'd bite too deep? Misty assures that she knows how far to bite down, how gentle to be (which she is all the time) and how much to take as well as how to comfort the person to a almost hypnotic state that they rarely ever feel it. Misty has only a top fang & a bottom fang that she uses carefully to puncture the skin & vein, to get what she needs. A risk of bleeding to death? NEED NOT worry about that. There are 2 types of veins she's aware of that are of concern. 1 is the ARTERIES (MAIN). The other is the smaller veins. These are the ones she get it from. Small vein blood tastes alot different from main artery veins. It is much thicker & has a hotter taste.

Each persons blood does NOT taste the same. Some are hot, some are salty, others have a strong vitaminy taste. These are usually the ones whom we call the HEALTH FOOD nuts.

My bites are NOT GAPPING holes as seen in DRACULA films, but merely HALF MOON SHAPED small marks (usually 2 close together) in which blood is extracted through the holes, they close after feeding because the suction on the skin draws it shut, the wound is cleaned, then doctored in case anyone fears to be infected. By the next day or same evening (hours later) the marks appear to be like a tiny rash mark or a small bug bite. I take great care when biting not to hurt donor, or cause any discomfort. I will not bite if donor is tense, or will not relax even after working to relax them after a period of time. I will give them a break (1/2 hr if allow) and try again later. If still no success, I either forget that person or if the person is known to me, will tell them to come back the next day.

Misty has insisted repeatedly that being bitten by her is a painless experience, but it has to hurt like hell. Even if she uses only two "fangs" (which must be tremendously awkward, but Misty has to do it the way they do in the movies), clearly the amount of pressure needed to break the skin will cause considerable pain, even if Misty has first given her donor a neck rub. In fact, a tearing action is probably necessary to get the blood to flow freely. She'd do better to use her front teeth, which are much sharper, and designed by nature for biting. Either way, the resulting marks are unlikely to look like a tiny rash mark or a small bug bite.

A human bite is dangerous, more dangerous than most animal bites because of the large amount of bacteria in the human mouth. It's fortunate that this modern-day vampire brings a first aid kit with her. Many vampires consider neck biting to be a very dangerous activity because of the location of the jugular vein and take their blood only from other parts of the body, but Misty got her ideas about blood drinking from Dracula movies, and Dracula bites people in the neck. Some of her donors insist that she bite them elsewhere, such as the bend of the arm or the wrist. Sometimes donors, feeling that a quick cut from a razor or a sharp knife will be much less painful than being chewed on by Misty, will cut themselves. Others will withdraw blood with a syringe. Misty insists that they do it out of her sight since it makes her queasy. "When I see the needle go in, I can feel the pain. I can feel what they're feeling, and it just makes me cringe," she said.

Misty tells the story in the red pages of one unusual donor:

> I remember one fella whom claimed to be a wolfman (he was terribly hairy) by night (every-night) when I was introduced to him, he wanted me to bite him & he wanted to bite me. Strange feelings arose, I got nervous & left. 3 Days later (evening time) I had to take 2 of my friends back over there because they knew the guy & he could get them passes to the CONCERT (in town) because he was a ROADIE for the band. I dreaded it. He came out of the house "Misty, come in." SO

I went in. He sat down on this couch & told everyone else to SIT DOWN!

Being invited by him personally, I guess I felt better, besides it was my 2nd time going there. He said "Don't worry, I won't bite you." My friends actually got swallowed up in the sofa which was over stuffed & the bottom springs had given away. They laughed as they tried to crawl out of the thing. I sat in a chair. He took me by the arm, led me to the bedroom, sat on his WATERBED, told me to sit.

"Now, I want you to bite me!" He insisted. I said "You don't give up, do you?" I said. He shook his head no. I had trouble the first time, I got a mouthful of hair! I finally located a spot on his neck with hardly no hair. I bit, he pulled me towards him "BITE me again & again & again!" So he was bit in 5 different areas of the neck, he wanted more, but I was all fanged out. Besides, I couldn't take in anymore if I tried. We walked out into the livingroom, my friends smile "have enough?" They seen my face wasn't so happy. "What's wrong?" they asked. "Please, no more tonight. I'll puke." I said.

One donor actually asked Misty to kill him:

AT the request of a donor, she dressed in black along with a long flowing cape, candle lights instead of lights in the darkened room, she walked across the room towards him. He lay back, she gently lay beside him. Relaxing him enough to pierce the flesh, she finally bit him making the blood flow easily. He moaned a slight bit, she pulled away, "Are you alright?" she was concerned. He smiled, "It felt so good like I was in a dreamland. No pain, but I could feel my life flowing into yours. Please continue." He told her assuring there was nothing wrong. She glanced over to see if it was affecting him sexually, it hadn't. She was relieved. As she continued, he pulled her to him, "KILL ME. TAKE ME. I'm yours." She felt insulted, jerked away & left, never going back. He wanted her to take his life. She refused. He must've been a LOONEY! Either that or he reached a high & didn't care. "I can not kill anyone. I do not have it within myself to do so." SHE tells people. There's no shame, no hidden quivers no smile when she says this, but the stern serious voice telling of her feelings, you know it's the truth by the tone of her voice. Before she'd hurt anyone, she prefers to hurt herself if need be, & believes in life.

She says she would never hurt anybody, but if she did kill somebody she would kill herself to escape punishment. "Well, if I ever went out and I killed somebody, I could live with the guilt. But most definitely I would destroy myself, otherwise I'd be hunted down, and I don't want that fear and have to go through the pain of maybe somebody driving a stake through my heart or something. They see these stupid movies, you know. Or be shot at with a bunch of bullet holes. No, thank you," she said.

She adamantly insists that her teeth aren't filed or capped, although people who know Misty told me a dentist made expensive, fanglike caps for her:

THESE FANGS are my own. INFACT, as a child, the dentist she was taken to had began to file them flat because she was cutting up the inside of her mouth & making it bleed. This was accidentally happening when she'd chew her food, which was another reason she was a slow eater. After she was coming out of the NUMBING GAS realizing he was flattening the tips of her fang like teeth, she jerked away & got out of the chair. "Leave my sharp teeth alone!" she yelled. She never returned to him ever again. It also made the dentist mad, he yelled back "Don't ever come to my office again!" The reason Misty went to the dentist was due to a broken tooth, exposed nerve from trying to chew a guitar string in half. She soon learned, YOU DON'T CHEW ON WIRE! She used to open pop bottles with her teeth until she broke another one of her teeth & had to have it fixed. Her fang like teeth were strictly for biting meats & for the purpose for feeding only, nothing else.

Misty claims to be very sensitive to sunlight, becoming nauseated when she's out in the sun for any length of time. She says she always wears number 15 sunscreen and claims to have fainted from the heat of the sun more than once. Bright light bothers her, too. "I have to wear sunglasses during the day," she said. "My eyes are very, very sensitive. I have dim wattage volts in my home, or I use candlelight."

Misty says that she gains the benefit of the immunities of the person whose blood she has drunk, and those immunities protect her for a few days. Scientifically, there is absolutely no evidence for this or for the supposed youth-giving effects Misty claims to get, and she certainly doesn't derive any strength from the blood she drinks, except possibly psychologically. Blood passes through a person's digestive system without being metabolized. She may call it feeding, but no calories or nutrients are absorbed. It's feeding of a different kind.

Misty also claims that she can tell when another person is sick and so she has no fear of contracting any disease from her blood drinking. A sick person smells like "pussy," she said, and further denigrated the smell of female genitalia by saying, "It's an odor almost like a death smell sometimes."

When she can't find a donor, she gnaws on her arm, drinking her own blood. "I can't bite myself on the neck," she points out. "Sometimes there have been situations where I've had to feed on myself for a day or two, just something to hold me over, but it doesn't do any good. If my immunity system is low, I'm not getting anything from myself, so I try not to. But there have been times when I had to, because I was too weak to do anything. I would stay home and sometimes people would come over and donate, and sometimes they wouldn't. So I had to drink my own blood, even if I got very little benefit from it. I had to."

Misty is well known in vampire circles. Still always remembering the warning words of her grandfather, she is downright paranoid about vampire hunters. She seems to think there are many such deranged people, and she takes certain simple precautions, such as receiving her mail at a post office box. She does receive actual threats, and it is difficult to judge the seriousness of them.

"A couple once wrote to me and told me they

needed a pair of vampire's eyes so that they could rule the world," she told me. "They said that if I didn't send them my eyes in two weeks, they would come and get them. Did they really think I'd be stupid enough to pluck out my eyes and send them to them? How could I see to address the box if I didn't have my eyes?"

The couple never turned up. But Misty can't keep her mouth shut and the police have dropped in on a number of occasions, asking about the homemade coffin in her house, telling her they hear she drinks blood.

"I nearly got locked up as a loony," she said. "A kid who worked for me knew I drink blood and I guess he told his parents. He used to call me mom all the time. Everyone gets close to me, they go, mom, mom. They didn't like the idea of him coming around me. They called the police and told them I was a vampire and drinking their son's blood. The cops tried to corner me. They got this little wooden coffin from a funeral home; I know they borrowed it. The head detective guy comes in and he goes, 'Does this mean anything to you?' He puts the coffin down in front of me. I go, 'Oh, that's pretty nice.' I liked it. I liked the shape of it; it was really neat. I said, 'That would make a good conversation piece.' I guess he was disappointed because he didn't get the response he was looking for. There were no charges. The boy never did give me any blood."

She talked her way out of it, but her desire for attention conflicts with her desire for secrecy. Misty claims that she speaks out about her blood drinking because she wants people to know that vampires are people just like everybody else, except that they need to drink blood to survive. During our conversations, it became apparent quite quickly that attention was what Misty was really starving for. Within half an hour of our first hour-long interview, she called back and informed me that there was more she wanted to tell me. This was the beginning of a bombardment of telephone calls and letters. One letter sported a blood-stain. Misty circled it and wrote next to it, "It's mine." The letters and telephone calls continue to this day, giving me a true understanding of what a vampire really is and what it feels like to be drained by one.

She admits to being unhappy and lonely, and says that she doesn't like to be around other people because when she gets involved it starts fights. Yet her self-description contradicts such tendencies.

"I'm a very nice person," she said. "I'm easy to get along with if you like me. I know I do things a lot differently than some people do, but that's just like if everybody was the same it would be dull. My goal object is to make people happy. That's the type of person I am."

In the red pages, Misty wrote of herself:

MISTY—an easy going person, sometimes shy. Loves to be where there is fun and rides. Loves animals, peace, flowers, bright colors, art & varied types of music including BACH STUFF. The towns people started calling her COUNTESS or Vampira back in the early 1970s. Being a person who love to listen to the CB radio, they called her "COUNTESS" instead of her handle she had picked which was The Flying Horse. She dropped out from listening to the CB radio late 1979 due to foul language & music players over the air. The Countess lost interest in the radio because some JERK out there was ruining it for everyone & wouldn't hardly let anyone talk.

Some knew what she was, called her many names such as The Daughter of Darkness, Dracula's Bride, and Vampira. She became very angered and they soon stopped calling her that. They found another name that didn't seem to bother her, & they said it fit her because she has a love for VICTORIAN HOMES & DRESSES . . . They started to calling her "COUNTESS." The name seemed to stick, she didn't mind. After being called COUNTESS for 3 YRS. over the CB RADIO, she decided that this would be her CB NAME & a nickname. This is how her name came about. It was not of her own picking. For some reason, the Name seems to fit the Countess with her mysterious ways & enchanting movements when she encounters.

Misty quotes herself: "I love the wilderness & all the wild animals running in it. It is a sign of untouched peace, something GOD made special to enjoy. Peace to me is animals running free, no corruption within open meadows."

The red pages continue: "She loves everyone. This is to ensure you how she feels about things. When animals or people are hurt, SHE cries. When they die, she's hurt."

She claimed to have two wolves, but it is illegal to keep wolves as pets and the authorities visited her soon after she bragged about her wolves. She denied that they were wolves, saying they were only huskies, and they must have been only huskies because she was allowed to keep them. She claims to have had a boa constrictor and a python, several lizards, and various fish, and, of course, to have raised bats.

She also has a cockatoo. When she first got the bird, it bit her. "I hit it so hard it crashed against the wall. I thought I had killed it. But it never bit me again," she told me proudly. Considering her background, it isn't surprising that such brutality comes easily to her. Another vampire told me that Misty claimed, in a letter, to drink blood from chickens and pigs, withdrawing the blood with a syringe, an experience no doubt painful and terrifying for the animals. She admitted to me that she's drunk animal blood, but said it "does not have what's needed." Still, she insists that she loves animals and that they're like her children to her.

In the red pages, she describes her interest in arts and crafts:

MISTY enjoys drawing or oil painting, does a very good job at it. MISTY has many hidden talents in which she usually keeps to herself. When she gets depressed or bored, she plays records, either draws or paints, or invents a new toy never seen or heard of.

"I prefer to do something CONSTRUCTIVE, rather than destructive when I am depressed or bored. I have found this to be a safe & great thing to do, even healthy thing to do according to many psychologists. INFACT contact anyone of the Dr.'s about this type of thing & ask. You'll find they all agree with my method." Misty says with a smile.

She also likes to sing. Misty's specialty is rewriting songs, giving them new, vampiric lyrics. Thus, "Hotel California" becomes "Hotel Vampira," "You Light Up My Life" becomes "You Bite Up My Life," and "Tonight's the Night" becomes "Tonight's the Bite." She sent me a very funny tape in which she simply sang her vampiric version right along with the original songs, in a clear, enthusiastic voice.

Misty's creative activities, while offering her some solace, haven't really improved the quality of her life that much. She says she doesn't have many friends. Instead, she has created an extended family of sorts with her group, appropriately named the Lost Shadows Gang.

As she tells it, "I started a group of my own in which I am a leader of this group. We protect each other. When we get together we have our meetings; we talk what's on our minds. It's just like your basic group meetings. You go out, you talk what's on your mind; you help each other out. We go out and enjoy ourselves, go bowling.

"These guys are a fun bunch to be around, because they like to sit around; they'll talk, and we'll joke with one another. If we got something on our minds, we all sit and listen. It's like one big happy family. In fact, they even call me sis. All of them wrap their arms around me and go, sis, sis."

Not all the members of the Lost Shadows Gang live in the same town as Countess Misty, so their bowling and arcade forays are limited. She started the group through an ad in *Fangoria,* a fan magazine for horror buffs. The group is of central importance in Misty's life, and since most of the members are in their late teens or early twenties, she actually does have a leadership role. In fact, she sends out bloodred Christmas cards signed, "Countess Misty, their leader."

She described the importance of the gang to her in a letter:

"I became weakened 11-6-89. All my boys (some group members) were concerned and had to be at my side and offer help, or they called with concern. They said, 'Please get better. We need you. We want you around. We don't know what we'd do without you. You've given us so much, so Much more than we could ever repay.' It was encouraging words. I knew they cared. I was in need. I finally had a chance to feed. I felt better hours later—I'm OK now."

All have protective "code names." Some evenings members of the gang will go out with Misty, some on their motorcycles, wearing patches on their jackets saying DEATH WAITS IN THE NIGHT! A group of regular donors gives them blood, but they're always looking for new blood. Sometimes they'll bring blood, in baby-food jars, back to Misty's house and mix it with coffee, wine, or beer in lieu of drinking it straight.

In the red pages, Misty thoughtfully provided more information about the Lost Shadows Gang, perhaps influenced by teen magazines.

EAGLE

18 Yr. Old young man, slim, very keen at sensing things, very shy. Enjoys the night. Loves parties, joking around, motorcycles (doesn't have one), NO TATOOS, likes dark colors, nice, quiet. Most of the time relys on others to get his need for him.

(She added in a letter, "Eagle gets his need once a week, very little.")

Doesn't like his picture taken if he can avoid it. Works in gardening. Isn't a couch potatoe, not afraid of work. Loves Misty like a mom, yet respects her as leader of LOST SHADOWS. Why was he called EAGLE? His face (nose & eyes) resemble the looks of an eagle, & his quick sense of awareness. Doesn't take drugs.

MARCOS
Almost 19 Yr. old young man. A male who girls seem to be drawn to. When I say girls, I am talking female, women of age. Jokes a lot, loves to laugh. Listens to alot of music, loves night walks. PARTY ANIMAL, no drugs involved. Loves action movies, likes the sight of blood. Has sex with donors when he feeds. MARCOS look almost like ALEX WINTER in the movie, THE LOST BOYS. Marcos works digging ditches, painting houses, & some construction work of sheds & etc. Marcos will ride motorcycles, but doesn't have one. MARCOS has NO TATOOS. Would like to have MISTY as a girlfriend, but she refuses. He too respects her as head of LOST SHADOWS. Bites his donors. Will help others to get their needs.

DAVID
Long Blonde haired Canadian born male, age 23 yrs. Tall, likable guy. Has a band of his own, plays gigs at clubs & etc. Plays guitar, rock N'Roll —METAL. Likes Guns N' Roses, Poison. Listens to music alot. Collects old time cars (models). Bites or cuts donors while making love. Very gen-

tle. Sings. Loves motorcycles (harley Davidson),
wears black, has several tattos.

FANG
22 Yr. old male, kinkish hair, nice smile. Re-
tractable fangs. Bites donors. Will play guitar
from time to time. Sings. Has a tattoo, very pale
skin. Listens to alot of King Diamond, Alice
Cooper & Poison music. Loves the color Black.
has a black coffin (keeps it hid). Also listens to
BACH. Bed sheets are satin Blood red in color.
Finds donors in Bars & party places. Other Nickname: DR. SYN.

BLACK WIDOW
Pale skin female, stays to herself most of time.
Night walks are her favorite. Listens to varied
types of music up to Soundtracks. Stays close to
home, very gentle, very likable person. Very sensitive towards people. Collects stuffed toys, odd
N Ends for her bookshelf. Loves long flowing
dresses that fit comfortable. Her feeding habits—
she says are personal. She cares for just about
anyone she comes in contact with that she's
friends with. Respects the group. Seems to be
happy all the time, loves animals of all kinds, is
against anything that contains any kind of animal
product, is not a meat eatter. She eats vegetable
foods only. NO TATTOOS.

GRIMM REAPER
Named this because he constantly wears black,
into heavy metal music, plays guitar or drums.
Rides motorcycles, loves to do dangerous stunts.

24 Yr. old male. long black hair, dark eyes. His smile sometimes sends a chill up your spine, esp. when he laughs. He purposely makes his laughter sound evil at times. He's a good person to know. Loves to date women, is gentle. Wears heavy steel toe boots. Keeps coffin hid away, only seen at night when he takes walks or rides bike. He works as a night watchman for a construction company. Has NO TATTOOS.

DOUGG

Also called DOUGG THE BUG. Is a Veteran, now has long dark hair, wears glasses that make you think of him as a bug. Rides motorcycle all the time (HARLEY), black boots & vests are his favorite items besides motorcycles. Quiet person, usually keeps to himself. Listens to 1970's music. Talks about the war alot. Smiles sometimes. He helps out if work needs to be done. The war left him slight disabled. Strong mind & will. INTO reading books of WAR & etc. A definate BOOKWORM. Another reason called DOUGG the Bug. Has fangs of his own, sometimes bite.

BONES

BONES got his name from his features of face & body. Pale skin, tall, accent, blonde hair. Loves Ozzy, Metallica, & metal music. Smokes cigarettes, trying to quit the habit. He's 18 Yrs. old. No girlfriends yet. He enjoys being by himself. Canadian born. Will work if have to, but would rather be a couch potatoe. Smart, loves to read, walks & moves fast. Mixed blood with beer a few times. Loves to party, likes wolves, black cats.

His favorite saying, "That's cool" or "That's fresh." Loves movies: action, fantasy & horror. Likes puzzles, cards, & few other games. NOT camera shy. Talks fast so anyone listening must listen good. Hates to repeat himself twice. Loves motorcycles, wants to buy one. No TATTOOS. Loves to take LONG WALKS night or day. Loves candle lights. Will speak his mind if he has anything to say. Gets very quiet when upset. Non-violent person, rather walks away instead of fighting. If cornered, will fight. Disapproves of any man hitting a woman. Respects Misty & loves her like a mom. Restless at nights, can't sleep, esp. during full moons. Enjoys riding with Misty when she drives around. Loves motorcycles, doesn't like crazy stunts like Grimm Reaper. He enjoys any & all gifts anyone gives to him.

In a letter she added, "Bones is very active. Times vary. Some days—daily, after 1 week of daily, he skips a day, then feeds. This goes on for 1-2 weeks & then back to daily. HE feeds only when he needs it, NO other time." When I asked Bones why he drank blood, he said, "It's different."

Misty is proud of the Lost Shadows Gang and her influence over the young vampires. She believes in conventional morality, and blood drinking does not violate that morality. Her convoluted thinking allows her to say that she lives a "clean" life. She strongly opposes drug use, doesn't smoke cigarettes, and claims to not drink alcohol, although in several letters she mentioned being so upset that she had a couple of drinks. She strongly dislikes homosexuals, calling them "fags," and claims that a judge who scolded her once when she was in court regarding custody of her children did so because he was gay. She gets very upset when she hears what she calls "foul language."

She dabbled in witchcraft at one time because there was blood drinking in the rituals. "Of course, they had their sex orgy thing afterwards. And I said, 'No, thanks.'"

Misty has had some serious problems with men. On top of all her other misfortunes, including uncaring men who slept with whores, spending their paychecks on them, Misty says she was raped three times.

"And so I have a thing towards guys. It's like a fear, and I don't have a sex drive like other people do. Whenever someone tries to get close to me, I get scared and I just back off. I don't have no desire. I don't go around messing around. The only time I had sex was with my mate," she told me.

As she told me her story, though, it became clear that, even though she believes she should only have sex with her mate, she has had sex with other people. When Lost Shadow Bones told her he was in love with her, she immediately opened her arms to him, eventually allowing him to move into her house. Marcos, who considers himself a ladies' man, was furious.

"Why didn't you do it with me?" he demanded. "I could teach you how to French kiss."

"You put your tongue in my mouth and I'll bite it off," she told him.

Young Marcos is a frightening guy. During a telephone interview, he told me that his first experience with blood drinking took place as part of a Satanic ritual. It is to Misty's credit that Marcos has left Satanism behind. He's very enthusiastic about blood drinking, loving the hot, thick, salty fluid, saying it tastes "so gooood!" Eighteen-year-old Marcos has an older, married girlfriend who has given birth to his child. He says he loves her, although he doesn't envision them together. He's drunk her blood, but doesn't anymore, because he's in love with her. He feels as though he's hurting a woman when he drinks her blood, since he bites her, and he doesn't want to hurt someone he loves. "I'm kind of sensitive," he said.

Misty told me in a letter, "Marcos is having trouble with his biting. He causes pain, sometimes 'painful' pain. He asked me to teach him my method of Hypnotizing the Donor & how to be gentle and all." Never one to lose a chance to keep a Lost Shadow near her, Misty continued, "I told him #1. Rome wasn't built in one day. It's take time to teach him & for him to learn. He's willing to do so. I'm glad he asked for help. I enjoy helping my boys. 'Boys' is a term used for MALE GROUP Members. 'Girls'—female members."

Marcos has no trouble finding people to get blood from. It's not really accurate to call them donors, since he finds them at parties and gets them when they're "off guard." "They're drunk out of their minds," he said. "They want to fuck anything that walks, so you just go up to them and say, 'What's up?' The next morning, I'm gone."

It's Mr. Goodbar come true. A girl is drunk at a party, and young, blond, baby-faced Marcos goes home with her. The next morning, she wakes up alone, possibly unable to remember the wild and bloody night, with a bad bite, sometimes on her neck, sometimes on her breast, sometimes in a place a lot more sensitive and intimate. Marcos claims he doesn't even leave a scar, but these vampires have a habit of underestimating the damage their teeth can do. He claims to "feed" every night, but isn't worried about getting any of the sexually transmitted diseases common these days.

"We all have to die sometime," he said.

"You don't care if you catch anything?" I asked.

"No, I don't," he replied.

"That's a weird attitude for someone so young," I commented.

"I'm not that young," he replied.

He says it makes him feel better to drink blood. One day he'll be "dragging" and the next day, after drinking blood, he feels "like I'm on acid or something! I get such power from it!"

Misty may think she is promoting safe and responsible vampirism with her Lost Shadows Gang, serving as a fine example by keeping the Lost Shadows away from drugs, but what she is actually doing is serving as an inspiration to young men who already have dangerous tendencies. Marcos and Eagle, his half-brother, were both in trouble for what Misty describes as "fighting." At the least, Marcos may sooner or later face assault charges, when he bites someone a bit more assertive whose memory is intact in the morning. The police, who are already keeping an eye on Misty, surely are aware that a bunch of tough kids are hanging out with the local vampire.

It would take great courage for her to admit that it's not blood she craves, but love. She doesn't want to give up her identity as the "mysterious" Countess Misty, and become just plain Linda Smith or Penny Johnson. Without it, she'd be an ordinary, overweight, anemic, and somewhat lonely woman. One psychiatrist who read Misty's letters and interviews thinks that her vampire fantasy holds her ego together. Without it, he thinks she might become psychotic.

Misty does admit to having talked to various psychiatrists. She told one of them that she drank blood, saying, "There's a reason why I don't go out and get involved in these active things like your tennis club and all these things. I can't stand being around a crowd of people. I drink blood." He became terrified, put some chairs between them, and sat on the other side of the room. From then on, she claims, he would always stay as far away from her as possible during her sessions. "He's scared to death of me," she said. She once told an M.D. who was treating her for anemia that she drank blood. She claims his response was, "Well, you've got to take care of yourself."

This nice group of guys who hug her and call her "sis" are vampires who gather around the VCR for a showing of *Near Dark* or *Dance of the Damned,* which Misty says are the two most accurate vampire movies she's ever seen, bringing glasses of human blood to their chairs. A matching set of cheap, heavy, blood-drinking glasses stays at Misty's house, one for each Lost Shadow.

She is passionate about her devotion to the cause of "Vampire's Rights." In a letter, she said,

> I started LOST SHADOWS in hope to build up my life more, help others & show people—that either human or Vampire (Special Species) there are good in all of us. Just because the idea of "Lost SHADOWS" *GANG* doesn't mean Violent Acts & etc. . . . against the world, or that we are Satanists. We're not. There are good among Vam-

pires as there are humans. This is one of the reasons "LOST SHADOWS" had to be formed. I *want* to prove the World they are wrong about Vampires being "Evil Spawns of Satan" & etc. We all want a chance in life as everyone else. Alot of us (as for myself) had NO Choice of what we are, we were born into it, we didn't ask for it, we didn't ask to be born Vampires! We are Americans as anyone else. I'll continue to fight for Vampire Rights. . . .

After all I've said about us (Vampires & Group members) do I SOUND like a psycho case? Insane person? A Fetist? Someone who doesn't know anything? This a fantasy/fairy tale? NO WAY—Do you think I got this info from books? Do you think I think I got this info from movies? Not on your life!

We want to be accepted among Society & not locked up with the looney's. It's wrong to lock up or destroy what Society doesn't understand. This may be the reasons I was put on the godforsaken Planet to help people on both sides (human & Vampire). This must be why I was born Strong & domineering. *What are looks?* People are wrong to judge by looks alone/or rumors they've heard.

Most of the letters from Misty were chatty, telling me everything from what she planned to cook for Thanksgiving ("turkey drumlets") to what channel CNN was on in her town to how happy she was that the San Francisco Bay Bridge had reopened, even though she doesn't live anywhere near San Francisco. She was especially fond of telling me about car accidents that she had witnessed, always with bodies scattered everywhere, usually having missed, just by seconds, being in said accidents herself. Once she even drew a diagram of a particularly complicated accident, and she gleefully described the face of one of the victims as "hamburgered."

One day I received a telephone call from her. "Carol!" she said histrionically. "You won't believe what just happened! Oh, my God, it's so terrible! A girl just got hit by a car out in front of my house! She's dead. Nobody knows who she is. I went out to look at her under the sheet, but I don't know who she is, either."

She recently underwent a two-day psychological evaluation in yet another of her brushes with the authorities. She told me that the top score was 50 and she had scored over 50. She also reported that the psychologist told her she was perfectly normal, except that she was a little more intelligent than most people and that she had some fear because of the way she had been treated in the past.

"Did you tell him you drink blood?" I asked her.

"Of course not," she replied. "It's none of his business."

One day Evil arrived. Another kid, this one nineteen years old, Evil had read about Misty in an account of Misty's attendance at a Dark Shadows Conference. The story told of her having bitten some two hundred people, with a line outside her hotel room. All were eager for the experience of being bitten by a "real" vampire. Misty, to her credit, says the account is absurd. At most, she bit perhaps twenty people during that weekend and there was no line outside her door.

Evil, a young man living in a rural area a thousand

miles away, intrigued by the story and long fascinated by vampirism, wrote to the Countess. He told her that he was a misunderstood young man. He wanted to study parapsychology and his parents didn't want him to. She invited him to come and stay with her while he pursued his studies, telling him that she had a house and as long as he worked to pull his weight, he was welcome.

She first described him in a letter: "He's sort of a SHY GUY & he's seeking my help for several reasons. The guy is a loner, no one seems to like him, people always harass him, he has emotional problems at this time due to the stress of his parents. They was trying to get him put away in a mental hospital because he was wanting to go to college to learn PARAPSYCHOL-OGY. His parents do not want him to learn it."

Evil, who is thus named because he resembles a character named Evil Ed in the vampire movie *Fright Night*, wasn't very secretive about his plans. His parents read the chapter about Misty and were horrified that the Countess was going to have their son for lunch. They took him to a psychiatrist who told them to let him go, that he had to make his own choices. He was booted out of the house and got on the bus that would take him to Misty.

In other letters Misty further described Evil:

He truly cares about me, loves to hold me and rock me in his arms, he's short like me, sort of long hair, but will have it cut soon like "EVIL ED'S" in Fright Night. He loves to go Bowling. He's happy around me and I'm very happy around him.

He's someone whom enjoys music, wild life

(he's a member of GREEN PEACE), stand nearly 5'9", slim, an avid book reader, light hair & eyes. Loves to wear Black or Jean type stuff. Into "PEACE"—NOT WAR.

"NO More prejudices, no more wars, Peace to the whole World, Anti-Right Wing, Anarchy!" He's against Satanism, Wicca (WitchCraft), or any other kind of stuff dealing in Magic—He loves Comedy/Adventure Movies and books. Not too much into horror stuff. He sleeps over 10 hrs. Not like Misty. He's tried to keep up with Misty (the leader of LOST SHADOWS! & can't seem to do it. He tires before she does & she keeps going. Any activity she does, the others try, some almost last as long as she does, but they tire sooner. . . .

He's had alot of fun with group, Almost ALL of the members like "Evil." He (Evil) did have problems at first with "Bones" because he (Evil) wasn't Californian, wasn't very active, always talked about the way he did things back home. Shockingly—With Misty's Strict rules & demanding his ways to change in order to fit in the group, he finally allowed himself (after 1 1/2 months) to relax & go with the flow. NOW he has NO problems. He used to be TENSE all the time.

At one point, "Bones" pulled a knife, was gonna stick/cut "Evil" with it, Misty pulled hers, stepped between the two, told Bones to go ahead & stick her. A tear came to his eye, "I CAN'T. I CARE TOO MUCH FOR YOU." Misty said, "NO fights! You know the rules. We're supposed to be like family." He put away his knife, she put hers away. It wasn't long before Evil & Bones made friends with each other. Now they help each other when in need, share idea's & all.

Evil drank blood the very first day he arrived. He tried to live on blood, which other Lost Shadows procured for him, drinking as much as four cups a day, but he soon got sick, cut back on the blood, and began eating food again. When I spoke with him, he told me he was glad I understood about real vampires, not those mentally disturbed people who wanted to be vampires, but weren't, not really. His parents were right. Misty did have him for lunch and dinner as well. He served as a donor, another young man for the Countess to feed on.

Within two weeks, he asked Misty to marry him. She accepted. After all, he drinks blood and he loves to go bowling. What more could Misty ask for? He told his parents he had already married her. Misty and Evil asked me to come to the wedding and be a witness. I begged off. They're talking about moving away, to the country. Misty has just gotten a loan and is attending truck driving school. Hopefully, those truckers will watch their language on the CBs. It would be nice to believe that Misty will finally find a happy ending.

CHAPTER 4

If I'm remembered for nothing else, I'd like to be remembered for developing, indeed, revolutionizing the hand stake.

—SEAN MANCHESTER

In 1967, two sixteen-year-old schoolgirls were walking home at night after having visited some friends in Highgate Village, an attractive suburb of London. As they passed the north gate of Highgate Cemetery on Swains Lane, they looked in and thought they saw graves opening and people rising out of the graves. Or so they said—the girls eventually were interviewed at length by various newspapers and gained the kind of attention they never would have gotten had they not come up with this story. After the incident, one of the girls, Elizabeth Wojdyla, began having nightmares in which something evil was trying to come through her bedroom window at night, something with a deathly pale face, like the corpses she'd imagined seeing leaving their graves. Or so she claimed, which led her to an even greater notoriety.

A few weeks later, a young man was also walking down Swains Lane with his girlfriend. Suddenly, she screamed. Someone was standing behind the same north gate, just a few feet away from the couple. After she screamed, the someone ran away.

It's not unreasonable for someone to cry out when startled by an unexpected figure in a cemetery, but Sean Manchester, a young man with a strong interest in the occult, lived near Highgate Cemetery in Pond Square, near enough, in fact, to hear the scream. When he learned of the second incident, he considered it cause enough to begin poking around in the cemetery, and began gathering stories of sightings of what was then known as the ghost of Highgate Cemetery.

And there it began—a series of rumors and stories, fueled by the ruthless British tabloid press, who loved it, of course, until eventually the wonderful old Victorian cemetery was overrun nightly with "vampire hunters." Tombs were opened and defiled, and irreparable damage done. It was an elaborate hoax with many participants, some innocents with overactive imaginations, others thrilled to see themselves quoted in the local newspapers (or perhaps on television), and others bent on self-aggrandizement.

Manchester wrote an account of the events, which was published in 1975 by Frewin Publishers, Ltd. He disclaimed this account to me when I met him in London, saying that it had been censored. Later, Manchester wrote another version of the events in Highgate Cemetery, called *The Highgate Vampire,* published by the British Occult Society in 1985. (Sean

Manchester was then the president of the British Occult Society.) It is a fascinating book, and not just because of the wild claims Manchester makes about vampires and about himself, but also because of the florid way in which it is written.

Periodic sightings of the Highgate ghost/vampire continued and, in the summer of 1969, Manchester crossed paths with Elizabeth Wojdyla again. In his book, he claims that "her features had grown cadaverous and her skin was extremely pale. She appeared to be suffering from a pernicious form of anaemia." (Pernicious anemia results from an inability to absorb the vitamin B_{12} in the diet because of a deficiency of an enzyme in the stomach called intrinsic factor. It has nothing to do with loss of blood.)

Elizabeth also told Manchester that her nightmares had returned. She would dream that something was outside her window, but that she was unable to move. The something would approach her bed, and she would see what she thought was the face of a wild animal with glaring eyes and sharp teeth, but then she would realize that it was the face of a man, gaunt and gray, with the expression of an animal. Something cold would touch her. She would grow faint and remember nothing else.

Coming from a strict Catholic family, Elizabeth had recently left home, at a very young age, to move into a flat, largely to continue a relationship she had with a long-haired young man named Keith, of whom her father strongly disapproved. Manchester met Keith, who felt that Elizabeth was possessed, not depressed. It was Keith who pointed out some marks on Elizabeth's neck.

The photos of these marks have been widely discussed in vampire circles. Dorothy Nixon, a longtime vampire buff and cofounder of the Vampire Information Exchange, wrote a telling article entitled, "Comic Book Art, Engineering Principles, and the Highgate Vampire."

In part she observes,

Her case is suspicious on two grounds: First, both her nightmares and her extreme worn-out feeling can be fairly easily explained as having resulted from various personal traumae, such as leaving her ultra-strict parents in order to live with her boyfriend. Second, there are a few things wrong with her "vampire marks."

The main problem with them is that they are arranged vertically, not horizontally. There are three conceivable ways a stereotypical vampire could bite: (1) pinching the skin with the upper and lower fangs on one side of the mouth (as Van Helsing indicates upon examining Lucy in her coffin in Chapter XV of *Dracula*), (2) shoving in both uppers (the way snakes bite), or (3) shoving in both lowers. As it turns out, however, the second and third methods are physically impossible with an otherwise human mouth. The front of the mouth curves around much more than people think, which means that the incisors (front teeth) would get in the way—especially if the fangs are, as often portrayed in the comic books, curved inward and back so as to make it very difficult to bite an object the size and shape of the human neck.

But even the first method can be used only in a direction in which the skin is reasonably convex and/or elastic—have you ever tried to bite a flat surface? On the human neck, this leaves only the horizontal direction. . . .

So much for mechanical considerations. The notion that vampires have fangs and bite on the neck is by no means universal in the actual folklore. . . . It is primarily a Western literary convention. Where it does occur in Eastern European belief, it probably arises from the association between vampires and werewolves, since that is the way wolves are commonly thought of as biting.

As far as Ms. Wojdyla is concerned, the most charitable explanation I can come up with is that it was a psychosomatic phenomenon—a diabolical equivalent of stigmata, perhaps. This is, of course, not necessarily to deny that the required psychic state may have been induced by occult means.

Actually, her marks, described as . . . "two highly inflamed swellings . . . a tiny hole in the centre of each . . ." seem to me more like large over-squeezed pimples than toothmarks of any kind, psychosomatic or otherwise.

Actually, they look more as though they were created, very amateurishly, with makeup. Manchester challenges Ms. Nixon's comments in *The Highgate Vampire*.

When I met Manchester in London, he gave me a packet of photos for possible inclusion in this book, and several of them look as if they had been doctored. A photographic expert looked at them and noted that in one photo—with the descriptive caption, "The haunted icy path which runs from the North Gate to the once-infested catacombs at Highgate Cemetery. A figure stands where the undead was seen."—the figure has a felt-tip-pen blob on the top of his head, inking out for some unknown reason what appears to be a policeman's hat. A close look at another photo reveals the tight dot pattern typical of newsprint—Manchester seems to have lifted it from a newspaper.

In a color photograph captioned, "A recent photograph of Sean Manchester standing before his house (known as Byron House) deep in the English countryside," Manchester stands dandily dressed in riding pants and boots and a loose-sleeved shirt with lace cuffs, a favorite outfit of his. Yet, in one window, the tables of a restaurant are obvious. In fact, several waiters are visible.

The photos of Elizabeth Wojdyla have been challenged by others, too. Although I haven't seen the early edition of Manchester's book, others who have seen it told me that the bite marks on Elizabeth's neck in those photos are different than those in the photos in *The Highgate Vampire.*

Keith, however, was either extremely gullible or in the mood for a hoax. When Elizabeth supposedly got weaker, he summoned Manchester again. This time Manchester brought a copy of *Dissertatio de Vampyris Serviensibus,* written by one Professor Zopfius, an eighteenth-century authority on vampirism.

He read an excerpt of it to Keith and Elizabeth: "They slowly come out of graves in the night-time, rush upon people sleeping in their beds, suck out all the blood, and destroy them. They attack men, women and children, sparing neither age nor sex. The people attacked by them complain of suffocation, and a great interception of spirit; after which, they soon expire."

Manchester admits to being largely influenced in his beliefs about vampires by such writers as Professor Zopfius and Montague Summers, who gathered together many accounts of vampires in Europe. At the beginning of *The Highgate Vampire,* Manchester quotes a passage by Jean Jacques Rousseau that many vampire buffs are fond of: "If ever there was in the world, a warranted and proven history, it is that of vampires: nothing is lacking, official reports, testimonials of persons of standing, of surgeons, of clergymen, of judges; the judicial evidence is all-embracing."

It's quite true that in these many old accounts of vampires, the witnesses are often persons "of standing." Persons of standing have done some extraordinary things in history, including burning witches alive, or torturing infidels in the name of Jesus Christ, Allah, or whomever they happened to be fond of. These accounts are often hundreds of years old. The doctor who might say, firmly, "Yes, that's definitely a vampire" had not even heard of germs. The judge who confirmed that the corpse about to be mutilated was indeed a vampire may very well have believed in many other superstitions, never walking under a ladder or fearing black cats. Science was not at the foundation of these judgments—superstition and fear were.

These are the sources that Sean Manchester relies upon for his "expertise." Since Manchester believed that vampires are averse to garlic, crosses, salt, and holy water, Elizabeth was soon surrounded by crosses, and wore one as well, along with a handful of salt tied into a piece of linen hung on a cord around her neck. Her bedroom was sprinkled with holy water. Garlic was hung in the window and on her door. Keith was given instructions on what prayers to say should Elizabeth become restless in her sleep, an indication that the evil vampire was near, trying to dominate her mind, urging her to remove the garlic and crosses so that he could get in. Instead of a doctor or a psychiatrist, poor Elizabeth got Sean Manchester and superstition. She recovered, he says, although it's unlikely that anything was wrong with her besides separation anxiety and a suggestible boyfriend.

The stories about a "Highgate ghost" continued. The newspapers published account after account of people who had seen ghosts. People began to come to Highgate Cemetery in hopes of seeing the mysterious spook. Real, tangible evidence of Satanic rituals was found, including circles drawn with Satanic symbols, pieces of burned crosses, and, worst of all, dead animals, whose throats had been cut and whose blood was used in the Satanic ceremonies. It seemed clear that all the mysterious, darting figures and nocturnal activity around Highgate Cemetery was due to the use of the cemetery for Satanic rituals. Satanists often use cemeteries for such rituals.

But then Sean Manchester called the press himself and, introducing himself as a vampire expert and president of the British Occult Society, explained that the whole business was really due to the existence of a vampire. This led to a media blitz that propelled Manchester into the national eye. He announced to the press that he had chosen March 13, 1970, as the day when he and his associates would exorcise the Highgate Vampire.

He was invited to appear on the British *Today* show,

which aired at 6 P.M. on the day chosen for the exorcism. In addition to an interview with Manchester, assorted "witnesses" also said they had seen "something" in the cemetery. This was Manchester's moment of glory and it is on this moment, more of notoriety than glory, that he has made his reputation as a vampire hunter. When he described it to me, he said, with his characteristic grandiosity, "On that same evening earlier I had gone on live television and announced that a sort of desperate bid was going to be made to deal with this thing once and for all, and, for one brief moment, the nation held its collective breath."

A large crowd formed at the gate and the police soon arrived, using large searchlights to light up the old cemetery, since people were climbing over the gates and the walls. Manchester himself led a group of one hundred people through the cemetery to where he thought the vampire's coffin might lie.

Manchester was lowered by a rope some twenty feet through a hole into the catacombs of Highgate Cemetery, like some ghoulish Indiana Jones. Two others joined him and they searched the catacombs, finding three empty coffins. They lined each with garlic, sprinkled holy water inside, added a cross, and then poured a circle of salt around each. Young Manchester and a half-dozen of his "hand-picked" assistants remained in the area of the tomb all night. Nothing happened. In the morning, he went back into the catacombs. The coffins, not surprisingly, were still empty.

Things were quiet for a few months after that night of insanity, although the damage to the cemetery was continuing, as other so-called vampire hunters poked around in the night. But then a headless body was found in Highgate Cemetery, along with more signs of Satanic rituals. Manchester went back down into the catacombs on his rope and looked for the coffins he had covered in garlic and holy water. One was missing, or so he says.

Along the way, he had met a young woman whom he calls Lusia in his book. Lusia had apparently taken up sleepwalking, something she had never done before, and strangely kept heading to Highgate Cemetery. Manchester followed her one night and found that she went to the Columbarium, a part of the cemetery where Manchester decided the vampire must be lurking. He claims to have heard a low, booming vibration, and so he placed a cross between Lusia and the iron door she was facing. Lusia collapsed and Manchester and her sister took her home. She claimed the next day to remember nothing. She, too, turned up with "vampire bites" on her neck on several occasions.

Several photographs of Lusia are printed in Manchester's book. One frontal shot of Lusia shows a young woman with bleached blond hair, wearing a very low-cut dress. Her arms are pressed against her sides in such a way as to push her breasts together so that they are nearly in full view, making her look very much the brazen hussy. Manchester's caption reads, "Lusia, beautiful and innocent as a child, who fell prey to the undead." Indeed, this photograph is part of a collage on the cover of Manchester's outrageous book. Another photograph of Lusia shows her in skintight pants "sleep-walking" in her Highgate flat.

It was Lusia who led Manchester, through hypnosis (for Manchester, it seems, can do everything, including hypnotize people), to the new resting place of the vampire. He and some of his cohorts entered a vault belonging to one Charles Fisher Wace of Camden Road, 1872, and, after checking the inscriptions outside against the numbers inside, found that there was one coffin too many. The coffin that looked in the best shape was opened.

His description of what was found within, as it appears in *The Highgate Vampire:*

Ignoring the mood of foreboding which now engulfed us all, I stepped forward and, with heart pounding, raised the massive lid. My torch lit up in unnerving revelation the sleeping form of something that had long been dead; something nevertheless gorged and stinking with the life-blood of others, fresh clots of which still adhered to the edge of the mouth whose fetid breath made me sick to my stomach. The glazed eyes stared horribly—almost mocking me, almost knowing that my efforts to destroy it would be thwarted. Under the parchment-like skin, a faint bluish tinge could be detected. The face was the colour and appearance of a three-day corpse.

"It's newly dead," said one of my assistants, breaking the silence. But the vault was more than a hundred years old and there had been no recent admissions. As he spoke I took up a stake made of aspen and placed the point over the evil heart. . . .

I looked away from those burning-red eyes and raised the hammer to strike the wooden stake with all my might. My mind's eye prepared itself for the jets of crimson spouting high in the air at the sound of the stake being driven home in a dull thud. I say in my mind's eye because just as I held my breath to strike the blow my arm was seized by an assistant who pleaded with me to desist, saying that it would be sacrilege. "If what lies before us is an undead," I replied, "it would be an act of healing."

Manchester was prevented from mutilating the corpse that time. Later in his book he describes confronting the same vampire in yet another place, this time in the basement of a "haunted" house, where he then staked it once and for all. But at Highgate he had to settle for an elaborate exorcism, involving more holy water, salt, and garlic, which ended in his shouting into the vault, "Begone, thou hideous demon, unto thine own place and return no more to plague the children of Almighty God."

Manchester denies any interest in publicity, although he has willingly participated in documentaries, been interviewed repeatedly, and even staged demonstrations with a Red Cross dummy on how to properly stake a vampire. He has gone on lecture tours and claims to have demonstrated that Dorothy Nixon's engineering principles are not correct, despite her training in engineering, and that the marks on Elizabeth's and Lusia's necks are quite accurate. In his letters to me, usually typed on reprints of yet another article about him, he discussed his appearances on talk shows and little else.

When I mentioned Sean Manchester's name to various people in the vampire subculture, they always responded by becoming very angry or bursting into laughter. "You know, he claims to be a descendant of

Lord Byron," one told me. "He's obsessed with it. And he claims to be writing the sequel to *Dracula.*"

Four different sources told me a story about a letter that was sent out to some of the members of the Count Dracula Fan Club that claimed Manchester had been killed in a duel defending a lady's honor. The letter requested funds to bring his body back from France and to build a memorial to him.

One source provided me with a copy of the letter, purportedly signed by K. J. A. Garforth-Bles, Executive Assistant, British Occult Society, which read,

> You will no doubt be saddened to learn that the President of the British Occult Society has not recovered from a fatal wound inflicted at a recent duel. There is little one can say when a leader of such high caliber is cut off in his prime. Yet, despite his expert swordsmanship, a mortal blow reached his target. Many will find him guilty of taking unnecessary risks, but Sean Manchester felt an obligation to live dangerously—such moments of peril found him in his element.
>
> He was perhaps best known for his explorations into the unknown regions of nether worlds and haunted places where vampires and demons repose and, like a knight of old, he slew them in the ancient manner that despatches dragons. He opposed tyranny of all kinds and never tired in his relentless battle with black magicians and their ilk. He overcame evil not by ignoring it but going to meet it head on. This was his axiom by which he lived—and died.
>
> It was the only way for him. He was a great gentleman and chivalrous to friend and foe, cour-

teous to everyone, unwilling to be praised above
his fellows, and always bore himself with an easy
dignity. Indeed, he was more than a great gentleman, he was the very soul in which spirit and
flesh strive for mastery, the purest knight of
them all. The great evils he met in combat called
forth even greater virtues to counter them. He
put himself always at the service of those who
asked for his help. He was content to live dangerously, carrying his life in his hands and willing to
lay it down rather than break the code of honour
by which he lived or be faithless to word or
friend. This vigorous, eloquent, and romantic figure believed in valor and paid its ultimate price in
his thirty-third year. Many will mourn his passing; some will applaud it no doubt; but none will
be left unaffected by it. The world has lost a
brave and noble friend.

With the announcement, a letter informed the re-
cipient that Sean Manchester had fought a duel, and
died, at the Citadelle de Montreuil-sur-Mer in France.
A photocopied photograph of him lying on the ground
among flowers was also included. A request for dona-
tions read, "The British Occult Society now wish to
repay the debt to their late President by returning his
body to England and erecting a suitable monument at
Glastonbury—the place he loved above all others."

Manchester told me he has about three hundred
members in his International Society for the Advancement of Irreproducible Vampire and Lycanthropy Research, all of whom subscribe to a newsletter, *The
Cross and the Stake,* for £6 a year. He sells a few
books, but, as with most of these vampire organiza-

tions, there's probably not much money to be made, if any. The society is intended to research cases of "actual" vampirism, and before setting up our meeting, Manchester wanted to make it absolutely clear that he considers supernatural vampires to be very real.

The question of Sean Manchester's finances is interesting, because it, too, is an area where he makes grandiose claims that are pooh-poohed by everyone else. There is a rumor that he owns a tea shop in Highgate Village, although one vampire expert retorted, "Maybe he works in a tea shop, but I doubt if he owns one." Most people agree that his wife does have some money.

His favorite claim is that he is the great-great-great-grandson of Lord Byron, which is absolutely central to his belief system. There's no definite proof for this, either, but for a man who has been called "the purest knight of them all" in his own death notice, it obviously is not too terribly difficult to make the leap of belief that is necessary.

When I went to England to meet him for this book, Manchester was unhappy about not being paid for the interview, and demanded my promise that I would list his address and information on how to order his book in an appendix. We set up a meeting place. I asked him how I would recognize him.

"Oh," he said, animatedly. "Do you know what Lord Byron looks like?"

"Yes," I replied. "Somewhat."

"Well, I look just like Lord Byron. You know I'm his great-great-great-grandson, don't you?"

The next day I took a lengthy train ride to a London suburb, which I promised Manchester I wouldn't name, where he was supposedly exercising his horse, although sometimes he referred to his "horses." He was concerned that one of his many enemies might injure the animals. At any rate, he met me dressed in full riding regalia.

He does not look like Lord Byron. His hair is chestnut-colored and curly, worn quite long, and, minus the sexiness, he reminded me more of Robert Plant, the great rock vocalist, than of chubby-cheeked, full-lipped Lord Byron. If Manchester was thirty-three in 1982, the year one of the death notices was sent out, then he was around forty when I met him. He coyly and absurdly refused to tell me his age, although he did venture that he looks a lot younger than he really is. He appeared to be in his middle to late forties.

We walked to a small arcade of shops and went to an outdoor coffee shop, where we sat at a wrought-iron table in extremely uncomfortable wrought-iron chairs. It was no more than forty degrees, and it might have been in the thirties. The English cold permeates the bones the way no other cold can. Since Pan Am had lost my luggage, I was dressed in my traveling clothes, a light cotton knit dress, and I was very cold and uncomfortable during the interview. He wore a black leather coat with fur trim and warm leggings, but this "great gentleman" seemed oblivious to my discomfort, even though I was constantly shifting position and readjusting my coat in an attempt to cover my exposed legs.

The first thing he said to me after we identified ourselves was, "My car and driver were just here. I don't know what happened to him." This "vigorous, eloquent, and romantic figure" graciously allowed me to pay for his cappuccino and my tea.

Manchester was on edge. He didn't know if I knew

about the phony death notice and about his claims to be a descendant of Lord Byron. I said nothing. I just wanted him to tell me about what he believed about vampires, and what he was doing.

One would think that talking to a man who claims to be a vampire hunter would be fascinating, but Sean Manchester was an utterly humorless bore. He doesn't agree with anybody about anything, it seems. He started by explaining that Raymond McNally's and Radu Florescu's years of research were completely in error, that Vlad Tepes was not the figure on which Bram Stoker's Dracula was based. Rather, he claims that one Janos Hunyadi fits the bill much better, since he was a count, and Vlad wasn't, he was in the right geographic location, and Vlad wasn't, and so on, listing several other reasons why Vlad was not the inspiration for Dracula, ignoring the most compelling reason of all, that Vlad's name was Dracula, son of Dracul. At times he seemed to forget he was talking about a work of fiction.

He told me he was currently working on a biography of Lady Caroline Lamb. Gothic Press will publish it. He also told me he's writing the sequel to *Dracula*. I asked who was publishing it.

"Well, everybody wants it," he replied. "It has occurred to me that my own real-life experiences have been rather Draculesque. It would be, I suppose, an interesting exercise to draw upon my real experience and to authenticate, I suppose, continue Stoker's story, which was quite clearly intended to have a sequel. And since no one else has done it, and since I've been asked on several occasions to fill that task, that quest, as it were, as a sort of exorcism, I suppose. I will rid my imagination of those final flutterings in the dark which are still there, and perhaps making it a less painful exorcism than the vampire book was. It will rid the cobwebs in what will be essentially a work of fiction, but based very much on real life experience. In fact, I shall be drawing on a great deal which is recognizable to those who were there, not least of all myself. But it will be in the guise of and very much in the style and form of sequel, an authentic, but a definite, sequel.

"It will not be something I shall be going mad after. It's something I shall, as the mood takes me, return to, rather as one returns to a rather good book and dips into it. I'll be returning to this project, this manuscript, as memories flicker back. I have roughed an early story line and I've roughed out the genesis of the connection tale. But I don't want to know where it goes from there, because I want to discover that as I write it. I never want to know where my fiction leads until I've pictured it. I only ever do one draft, you might be interested to note. Except for grammatical or other reasons, I never do second or third drafts. I only ever put down a first draft and that's it. I would probably discover that the others would be inferior, or at least not satisfactory to me. I'd probably discover that I was much happier with it, even though it was more rough, I was much happier with what I was originally getting at. I don't mind a rough diamond so long as it's a diamond."

In fact, six months later, Manchester sent out a flier indicating that the book, now entitled *The Dracula Legacy,* will be published in 1993 by none other than his own Gothic Press. I tried to get him to talk about vampires.

"A vampire is fundamentally a reanimated corpse," Manchester said. "It is metaphysical in nature."

Manchester believes that the unwillingness of people to believe in vampires is what gives vampires their strength. And this disbelief hampers his ability to fight them. He says he has learned of the existence of about seventy vampires over a period of twenty-five years, but was unwilling to admit how many he actually has staked.

"You see, one is up against the problem that nobody in authority, the powers that be, much less the legal system, will admit to the existence of vampires," he told me. "You can't get away with bending, breaking the law by saying, 'Ah, but I was saving this community from contagion from a local vampire.' What you will end up with is being charged and probably found guilty of being in an enclosed area for unlawful purposes, damaging memorials of the dead, desecration and sacrilege, interfering with a corpse for an unlawful purpose, and mutilation of a corpse."

He brought up the subject of David Farrant, the only other person to have gained any real notoriety during the brouhaha at Highgate Cemetery. Farrant ended up receiving a jail sentence of four years and eight months for his activities at Highgate Cemetery, although Manchester believes that he didn't deserve the sentence.

His description of Farrant and his activities in *The Highgate Vampire* is striking in that it could so easily be a description of Manchester himself. He says, "In his attempts to attract the limelight, he had displayed all the symptoms of someone with an identity crisis. He adopted grandiose titles, boasts and promises which were to newspaper hacks what a candle-flame is to moths. But he never could deliver the goods and took to dangerously half-admitting things about which he knew nothing and had no part, so as to hold attention."

Manchester told me that Farrant was threatened by Satanists, and that he "was sucked into a dark, diabolical world. He lives a very lonely life in a multi-occupied room opposite Highgate Wood, an almost entirely reclusive existence, a pale, slightly humped shell of a person whose skin never appears to see daylight, with red eyes, and the usual appearance which goes with a not particularly healthy, warm, robust person," he claimed.

Manchester says Farrant ruined his own life, "against everyone's best advice, not least of all myself. I actually went on television and warned him in particular and many others in general, 'Do not even get involved, don't clamber over the wall in a free-lance capacity. Leave it to those who know what they're doing. This is as dangerous as interfering with a live electric cable. Leave it to those who know how to handle it.'"

Manchester says he does. "You've got to understand that I was born into this. I first learned of the actual lore, I suppose, at a very early age through a nanny bouncing me on her knee as she described her visit to the cinema where she had been terrified by *Dracula*—probably the Bela Lugosi version of it. I was, you've got to remember, brought up in the grounds of Newstead Abbey Park where my grandparents owned twenty-odd acres, in the shadow of my somewhat illustrious ancestors' once family home, Newstead Abbey.

"I was raised in an environment where I was gazing

almost daily at a semi-ruin which had a history of haunting and contained one of the leading gothicists, to whom I am connected by blood, in an area where there were many tales of ghosts and whatnot. We had ghosts of cowled monks and wenches in distress flitting to and forth.

"In the end, the reason my grandparents sold the lodge was because my grandmother, who regarded all of this as superstitious nonsense, was putting out some plants in the rockery one evening while waiting for her husband to return. It was quite late and she was terrified by a black phantom. On another occasion, in much the same circumstances, the dark specter caused her to fall down the rockery, where she lay for several hours until her husband came home. She had been so terrified by something she didn't believe in, the door to her subconscious had been ripped off its hinges, and she begged, after many happy years of living there, to get away. They did move, but she didn't live much longer. It caused some sort of cancer and she didn't survive. It literally frightened her to death.

"And I was brought up with all this going on. I didn't have a normal existence. I didn't have a normal education. I've had quite an unusual life, one where the unusual seemed to be made to measure for someone like myself. For me, what seems extraordinary and odd to others is second nature. It's only what I've always known. And I am most at home in old places, semi-ruined mansions, and baronial halls.

"I'm often confronted on radio and television, asked, 'Weren't you frightened, weren't you terrified when you were in the depths of the cemetery and opening this or that tomb and peering into that sar-

cophagus?' And the answer is simply no, no more than
a firefighter putting out a fire or a person working in a
nuclear processing plant," he told me.

As I watched the dissipated-looking man sitting in
his riding clothes, with his soft pink fingers peeking
out from a pair of unraveling fingerless gloves, I wondered just how many graves he had actually opened,
how many cold and musty catacombs he had examined, how many crypts he had broken into. He
didn't strike me as someone willing to put up with
such discomfort, to take the risk of being arrested.
Rather, he seemed more the type to sit around reading old books and then recycling what he had read
into books of his own, drawing upon his rich store-
house of hyperbolic clichés.

"For me, the pursuit of the unusual—to seek out
and deal with vampires and, for that matter, if necessary, kindred things like werewolves (they seem to be
less frequent)—is a job, is a profession to which I've
always given myself. Really, it's the only thing I've
made a career of. Yes, I am an author. Yes, I do perform at concerts my own compositions on piano. Yes,
I do give poetry recitals. Yes, I am also an historian,
and I'm interested in archaeology a little. Yes, I do
other things, mostly in the arts. But my occupation, it
has to be said, is largely that of vampire hunter."

He then opened a red leather briefcase, which contained a large silver cross wrapped in what appeared
to be a piece of an old T-shirt, and several short
wooden stakes, about a foot long, with a cross etched
into the top of each. They looked as though they had
been cut from the legs of a chair.

"If I'm remembered for nothing else, I'd like to be
remembered for developing, indeed, revolutionizing

the hand stake, which, as you can see, is light, easy to conceal on one's person even, but certainly in a small case or bag. Up until this century you will find that your average peasant, and indeed your bona fide vampire hunter . . . used the average sort of stake that was in general use, approximately three feet in length and very often as wide as three inches in diameter with a point. The thought of a vampire hunter today lugging around with him a three-foot heavy stake is quite preposterous. One just simply cannot go around with a quantity of three-foot-long, three-inch-diameter stakes. It's just not done," he exclaimed.

"Do you always carry a cross and stakes with you?" I asked.

"Well, I certainly always have a cross with me, but not always stakes."

The briefcase also contained three copies of *The Cross and the Stake,* which Manchester puts out as the official newsletter of his International Society for the Advancement of Irreproducible Vampire and Lycanthropy Research. "Irreproducible" means that you have to take Sean Manchester's word for it. He showed me a few specific items in the newsletters, but refused to give me any copies, saying that it contained the names and addresses of some members and was confidential.

I obtained a copy of this newsletter elsewhere and was not surprised to find it to be primarily a platform for Manchester's writings, full of advertisements for his books and tapes. The issue I saw emphasized his obsession with Lord Byron, who was on the cover in a likeness that did not, in the slightest, resemble Sean Manchester. Inside, a drawing showed where Byron's coffin was in Hucknall Church, followed by an account of the opening of Byron's vault in 1938. Next came one of Manchester's rough diamonds, a short piece entitled "Lady Caroline Lamb—Ghost, Demon, or Vampire?" followed by an update on the attempt to exhume the grave of Robin Hood, whom Manchester believes was killed by a vampire. The owner of the estate where Robin Hood is thought to be buried refuses to allow Manchester to dig Robin up.

It's the two pages of letters and classifieds column that Manchester didn't want me to see. The classifieds are especially interesting, such as: "The October 1987 hurricane left a wealth of material for quality wooden stakes. A stake, let us not forget, can only be used once. Seasoned stakes made to specific requirements by a master stake-maker." A note from the editor in parentheses says, "Hurry, while stocks last!"

Or, "I have been making investigations into the possibility of more vampires in the Highgate area and, quite frankly, am very worried about my scary discoveries. Will anyone assist me?" The editor's note here reads: "X's views do not reflect those of the ISAIVLR."

Sean Manchester believes that vampires are a huge problem, in fact that another vampire epidemic is due to strike. He even dared to compare it to the AIDS epidemic and nuclear war.

"The present age, with materialism, atheism, greed, wickedness to the fore, is absolutely ripe for a new night of the undead—a night rather like a nuclear winter which would last for a very long time. I see all the hallmarks. The ground is being laid by the revival of diabolism, black magic, witchcraft, and Satanism.

"They are," he continued, "through their own stupidity and foolishness, but basically through their own black power, corrupting the world with the most evil force and supernatural terror that has ever existed—the vampire. . . . In the past, we were slightly protected by our insularity, the fact that it would take many years for a plague to get from A to B, but now something which began in Africa contaminates the world almost instantly. AIDS is rampant and will kill off many millions. I put it on a par with that. But worse, it has a metaphysical, spiritual aspect which is more deadly than even the AIDS virus, because, if you accept nothing else in the Bible, you must accept that the spirit is channeled through the blood.

"The undead, the vampire, this monarch of all evil, this prince of darkness, is the progeny of Satan who is the darkness in the world and who will bring death and destruction. I suppose in a sense we're only seeing the beginning of something which is too horrible to even contemplate.

"And it remains for people like myself, of which there are not too many, shall we say, to remain ever vigilant, and when the time comes be prepared to restore that which was lost, like Arthur in his time, who was born into the dark age, who was able to unite those few around a round table, who were willing to quest and restore that which was lost, to bring peace, to protect the innocent, to protect those who couldn't protect themselves and to fight for right, not for might," he continued.

The whole time he spoke, a total of three hours on the wrought-iron chairs in the cold British winter, Manchester hovered over the tape recorder, carefully making sure that the tape didn't run out, very concerned that I not miss a single word. In addition to the disturbing lack of emotion in his voice, he almost never looked at me, instead staring off into space. Although I did manage to squeeze a few questions in, he spoke in an almost uninterrupted monologue, drawing together his vampire and knight-of-the-holy-grail fantasies, placing himself firmly in the center, the self-proclaimed great-great-great-grandson of Lord Byron. And yet in that three-hour outpouring of gothic excess, he never once came up with an original thought. It was all regurgitated fantasy channeled through a not very original mind.

"We're losing a lot at the moment throughout the world. We're losing our innocence, we're losing our heart, we're losing our soul. The age of romance is gone. The age of enlightenment is gone. The age of invention is gone. It is now the age of darkness," he said, only weeks after the Berlin Wall began to come down.

The good news is that Manchester thinks the forces of light will win. And he offers some tips on how to survive this horrible army of vampires when they come through your town.

"We are individually responsible," he told me. "Suddenly we're going to, each of us, be faced with a great reckoning. And there will be those of us who are prepared. We'll be able to amply cope with the immediate danger. I envy the innocent, the truly innocent, because they are saved. But for the rest of us, we must stand shoulder to shoulder with what we know to be right and true and good.

"People need to get their act together. People should immediately, instantly, embark upon a quest to discover themselves, and, in doing so, under the hammer blows of the danger, a higher quest will unfold. You cannot start with the higher quest. You must start with the quest for self-discovery. On that journey you will then discover the higher quest which is the cosmic quest for all," he said. "Most people are strangers to themselves and are simply automatons who are programmed to go through certain actions and are conditioned to think and to work in a certain way. They need to rediscover their lost innocence."

Manchester stopped to take a breath and I turned off the tape recorder, said thank you, and started to pack up. There was still no sign of his car and driver and he escorted me back to the train station, quizzing me on the way about who else I was going to see in England, generally trying to find out if I'd heard any stories about him. He left me at the station and, as he walked away, I was tempted to follow him and see where he went, but I was freezing and my jet lag was catching up with me.

A few days later, I went to Highgate Cemetery to see the scene of all the fuss twenty years before. I walked down Swains Lane, past the chained and locked north gate, where so many sightings supposedly were made. Highgate Cemetery is now owned by a private group known as Friends of Highgate Cemetery, largely members of the community who contribute time and labor to renovate the cemetery and keep it open to the public. They charge admission to both sides of the cemetery. The Eastern Cemetery is most famous for containing the grave of Karl Marx. An enormous sculpted head of Marx is the current monument on the grave. My guide told me that previous monuments had been blown up.

The Western Cemetery, where all the vampire hunting went on, is closed to the public except by tour. The Friends of Highgate Cemetery say that, since that older part of the Highgate Cemetery is in fairly poor condition, it is not safe for people to wander about at will, and the Friends can't get insurance if they allow it. Although nobody cared to go on the record, it seemed fairly clear that preventing the kind of damage that had been done twenty years before is also a strong reason for limiting access to the Western Cemetery. Sean Manchester, in particular, has been banned from Highgate Cemetery, and, although I would have enjoyed a tour from Manchester himself, I had to settle for the crusty, white-bearded, strongly opinionated guide.

At first I was the only tour member, so I leveled with the guide, telling him why I was there and what I wanted to see. He was very unhappy. Although a few people caught up with us later, he did take me by the Columbarium, where he spoke of the "depraved people who broke open tombs, tipped over urns of ashes, and desecrated graves."

It was then that the reality of what Sean Manchester had done or claimed to do really struck home to me. As I stood there in the beautiful old cemetery, where families had brought their loved ones to rest, erecting over them tombstones with such charming inscriptions as IN LOVING MEMORY OF SARA EMMELINE HOWE (QUEENIE) WHO FELL ASLEEP, and BESSIE SARAH ELIZABETH WAS THE FONDLY LOVED WIFE OF JOSIAH GEORGE DOREE WHO DEPARTED THIS LIFE AFTER LONG SUFFERING BRAVELY BORNE, I felt no fear, sensed no evil atmosphere, even though Manchester insists the cemetery has that atmosphere. It was an old cemetery, with many overgrown graves, and was full of wildlife, including foxes and many kinds of birds, which the Friends of Highgate Cemetery had wisely determined to be also worth preserving. In the right light, it would make a great setting for a vampire movie, and a number of them have been made there, but in this, the bright afternoon sunlight, it was a place of great beauty and peace.

The guide was right. Only depraved people could break open tombs, open coffins, and interfere with the remains within, perhaps even to the point of driving a stake into the body. It was Sean Manchester's activities, and those of the other "vampire hunters" drawn to the cemetery by his absurd statements to the press, that were clearly, in the bright of that afternoon, the true evil that occurred in Highgate Cemetery.

CHAPTER 5

Here I am, six hundred years old, and my manager thinks she's my mother.

—VLAD

Vampirism is about sex and power. So is rock and roll. The image of the vampire has made its way into many rock concerts and videos. Fangs dripping with fake blood have been attached to the eyeteeth of such theatrical heavy-metal performers as Ozzy Osbourne and Alice Cooper, whose song "Fresh Blood" is a vampire rock-and-roll classic. Blackie Lawless of WASP has been known to drink a skullful of fake blood when performing, and the members of Mötley Crüe have bitten many a fake blood capsule, allowing the stuff to drip disgustingly down their chins.

The now-defunct 45 Grave played up the vampire image in their lyrics, stage shows, and costumes, including the very funny song "Riboflavin Flavored Non-Carbonated Polyunsaturated Blood." Skinny Puppy, an industrial dance band, frequently incorporates vampire references into its lyrics, as well as samples from vampire films, such as Warhol's *Dracula*. They, too, use fake blood in their stage shows. The speed metal band Blood Feast offers the exhausting instrumental "Vampire" on one of their albums, and the song "Blood Lust" on another. Other clearly vampiric songs include "Night of the Vampire" by Grim Reaper, "Blood Banquet" by Mighty Sphinchter, and a number of songs by Concrete Blonde, including "The Beast," "Darkening of the Light," and "Bloodletting."

Bauhaus recorded one of the best vampire songs ever, "Bela Lugosi's Dead," which plays over the opening scene in *The Hunger,* during which two vampires, played by Catherine Deneuve and David Bowie, search for their latest victims at a dance club. Roky Erickson's "Night of the Vampire" is also one of the best, managing to be vampiric, original, and listenable all at the same time. The Legendary Pink Dots, on their album *Any Day Now,* include the spooky and compelling song "Casting the Runes," about the immortal Madelaine against whom people painted crosses on their doors, praying not to be her next victim. Helstar, a powerful, tight heavy-metal band from Houston, has created a superb album entitled *Nosferatu,* which is entirely based on the Dracula story, complete with audio samples from the Frank Langella film. Unfortunately, Helstar didn't receive much backing from their record company and the opportunity to make compelling videos was not seized.

A few of these musicians may drink blood. Rock and roll is about extremes and drinking blood is extreme. Although rock superstar Jim Morrison's lyrics weren't about blood-drinking vampires and he never wore a cape and fangs in performance, authors Jerry

Hopkins and Danny Sugerman, in their book *No One Here Gets Out Alive,* report that Morrison supposedly drank blood on at least two occasions. The first was during his Wicca wedding, when a few drops of blood from each partner were mixed into a consecrated cup of wine from which they drank as part of the ceremony. Another time, while flying on cocaine, Morrison drank the blood of a girlfriend, Ingrid Thompson, according to Hopkins and Sugerman. They also report that Thompson had told Morrison that sometimes she drank blood. Morrison was curious, so she cut her hand. Morrison caught the spurting blood in a champagne glass. He drank some of it and they smeared their bodies with the rest. When Morrison woke up the next morning on blood-caked sheets, his body streaked with dried blood, he was, for once, scared.

The vampire novels of Anne Rice are probably the most important cause of the current infatuation with the vampire in American society. Rice sensed the unspoken link between the throbbing music and the throbbing blood and made her character Lestat a rock star. The power and domination the vampire has over his victim is comparable to the power that rock stars have over their fans, sometimes reducing them to screaming, weeping, adoring creatures who can only offer their money and, if they get the opportunity, their bodies to these exquisite bad men.

Rice, in turn, has inspired more than a few rock musicians. Sting gives Rice credit in his liner notes for *The Dream of the Blue Turtles.* His song "Moon over Bourbon Street" is sung from the point of view of a vampire who, like Lestat, struggles with his need for blood, anguished because he must kill.

Vlad, lead singer, guitar player, and songwriter for the band Dark Theater, says that although he likes Rice's books, he had planned on having a vampire rock band long before he ever heard of her. Vlad claims to be a direct descendant of Vlad Tepes, the infamous bloodthirsty Rumanian prince who was known as Vlad the Impaler for his favorite form of execution, impaling people on pointed sticks where they were allowed to die slowly. Young Vlad thinks his ancestor has gotten an unfair rap. He may have been "nearsighted and selfish," but he did, after all, scare the Turks so badly with his hideous practices that they decided Rumania wasn't worth the fight. Young Vlad considers his ancestor a heroic figure whose main concern was the protection of Rumania.

Vlad's brother has traced the family genealogy all the way back to a maiden raped by Vlad Tepes. But young Vlad also believes he is the reincarnation of Vlad Tepes, and that he has been reborn continuously down the family line. "It's a soul progression," he explained. "A soul runs through a lineage. Certain souls keep progressing through the centuries and they retain the majority of their original characteristics, passing them down through a family." According to Vlad, he is his own grandfather and will be grandson to his present self.

"There are things I can remember from previous lives," Vlad said, "but there's a lot of blank space, too. To me, it's all the same life. There are things that I would really have no way of knowing that I know.

"We are a very old line," he explained. "It's not like the reincarnation of Buddhism or Hinduism, where the purpose of each life is to move on and on to higher consciousness until you finally reach Nirvana. That sort of reincarnation is a stepladder, while mine is a continuation. I hope it will continue forever. My personality will be very dominant—I'm making very sure of that. Each time the life goes on, my character tries to gain dominance. That is true immortality, if I can erase whatever characteristics that would be in the body that follows mine and I can dominate."

Although his ancestor Vlad Tepes didn't drink blood regularly, he did do so on at least one occasion. Tepes scholar Dr. Raymond McNally found a document just a few years ago that describes Tepes dipping bread into a bowl of the blood of one of his victims.

Young Vlad claims to drink blood regularly. "I have to. I must drink blood in order for the core to continue. I do it to renew myself," Vlad said. "After all, in Vlad's age and ages before that, blood drinking was really quite a common occurrence. It was believed that if you drank the blood of an enemy, it would increase your own strength by taking the enemy's strength into your body. It's not like I look at people and say, 'Hmmm, cattle,' or 'Hmmm, a big pork chop. Tasty.' It's nourishment of the soul."

Even as a small child, Vlad was aware of his desire to drink blood, and he acted on it very early. "You do it in stages," he said. "You start with your own blood." When he was six, he and some friends who were playing Dracula decided to try the real thing. "I was a biter," Vlad explained. "If I would get into a scuffle, as young boys do, I would bite. I wouldn't hesitate." So he bit a friend's hand and sucked some blood from the wound.

"I caught a little hell for that one," he told me. "It was noticed. That's always been one of my problems.

I've always been noticed. As much as I've tried, lots of times, not to be noticed, it just happens."

It probably has something to do with his appearance. Vlad is pale-skinned and dresses only in black, of course, wearing his black hair long and tied back with a wide scarf. He's got a real baby face, round and plump-looking, and he's plucked his eyebrows and then redrawn them to arch upwards. Eyeliner emphasizes his small, dark eyes. Two rosebud lips balance out the eye makeup, although Vlad has shunned lipstick. He looks more like a pirate than a vampire to me, but these things are a matter of taste. One girl said to him after a show, "I wish everybody looked like you."

"When I was very young, I never really understood why I couldn't deal with sunlight. There were times, when I was very little, when I had to be taken to the emergency room because I had third-degree burns from being in the sun for an hour." Vlad's still very sun-sensitive and keeps himself covered whenever he's in the sun. His eyes are very sensitive as well, and he has to wear sunglasses when he goes out. He had eye surgery when he was very young. He doesn't have porphyria, a blood condition that can cause severe sensitivity to sunlight, nor is he anemic; Vlad's been tested. In fact, he's physically very healthy. The sun sensitivity runs in the family, although he thinks he is the only vampire.

As a teenager, Vlad was known as "Mr. Hickey." Hickeys do draw blood to the surface of the skin, so giving hickeys was a logical stage in his progression to active vampire. He is quick to point out that he doesn't take blood from anybody who isn't willing to give it to him. He hates the word "donor," though, saying that vampirism is spiritual and sensual, not clinical. People who give him blood usually find him "for some reason quite fascinating, or because it's a kick for them to be bitten because it's something unusual. It's not difficult to find someone to give you blood. Being a rock musician helps. Rock music is very vampiric, alluring, enticing, just like Anne Rice says.

"Vampires are no longer considered evil, ugly creatures of the night who turn into mist and steal into your bedroom at night and suck you dry," Vlad continued. "Now they're sexy and beautiful; they're Frank Langella. That's what it's turned into. Rock musicians always have groupies. I don't like to call them groupies. They're just people who are lonely and they see someone who is just so attractive and different that it takes them away from their normal world when they listen to the songs or when they go to the concerts. Vampirism is the same. When you combine the two, as Anne Rice did, you have something of great power."

He does worry about AIDS, a tough problem for a rock musician who is constantly being propositioned, or so he claims. "I get to know people for a long time —days and days—before I'll drink from them. No 'one-night bites' for me. I usually return to the same [donors], although some people don't want to do it again. It's not a painless experience, not at all. But whatever they get out of the experience, I want them to enjoy it. Generally, they do. There were some people who found it too painful. Some people wanted to be cut, rather than bitten—it's much less painful. But biting is probably the only part of the vampire fantasy I hold on to. It's not that important. It's just my preference. It's much more intimate. It's a very intimate act. I only bite women because vampirism does have a sexual component for me, although I don't become sexually aroused.

"My teeth are really sharp and I have very prominent eyeteeth. I have a tendency to bite my lip, so I'm afraid a cut in my mouth will make me vulnerable to AIDS," he explains. Ultimately, though, Vlad knows that "immortality is not of the flesh, immortality is of the soul." As long as he fathers a child before he leaves this life, his immortality will be ensured, since the line will be continued and he will be able to incarnate in the next child of that line.

"I drink more than the average vampire does, more than a glassful," Vlad said. "It doesn't make me sick or upset my stomach. I can tell what's in the blood. It's generally a metallic taste, much more so if the person is a heavy caffeine drinker or a heavy smoker. It tastes like you're drinking it out of a metal cup, a combination of bittersweet and metallic-tasting. It often depends on my mood.

"Drinking blood makes me euphoric, something a lot of blood drinkers say. It alters how I perceive things. My senses are very acute. It's not supernatural, they just are. It runs through my line," Vlad continued. "I'm not superstrong, though. I wish I was, that would be fun."

Vlad claims to be a "meatarian," that is, a person who eats only meat (in his case beef, not pork) and not even with a baked potato thrown in. He also eats what he refers to as "big game fish" but rarely eats chicken, since he doesn't digest it very well. Occasionally he will eat exotic fruits. But he probably wouldn't be caught dead or undead eating ordinary fruit, such as an apple.

Some people react very strongly to Vlad. He said, "Most people actually believe that I am Vlad Dracula," an absurd claim, since most people don't know who Vlad Dracula was. People do think he looks like a vampire. "People come up to me and say, 'I know what you are,'" Vlad said. "I deny it, saying, 'It's just an act; don't worry,' but they'll persist. They say they know because of my eyes, because I have very striking, intense eyes. The eyes are the portal to the soul. It's very hard to shake them once they do this. They want to be who they think I am. I've been offered incredible things to turn people into what they think I am and I try to tell them, 'I can't do that.' Someone will pull his shirt down and stick his neck out at me and tell me to go ahead and bite him, to turn him into a vampire, too. I would never drink from someone like that. That would be insane.

"I may be a vampire, but I can't turn other people into vampires, and I can't give them immortality. The few people who don't crave immortality are the luckiest people there are because they're going to be living their lives to the fullest, not looking for the next plateau of humanity that they can leap on and grab some miracle drug to do.

"I was once cornered by three guys who seemed to think Anne Rice's books were nonfiction. They knew her characters very well. They asked me, 'Do you know Lestat?' I said, 'Pardon me?' They asked, 'Do you know him?' I said, 'Well, I've read the books, if that's what you mean.' They said, 'No, no, no, do you know him?' Then one of them said to the others, 'No, he's more the kind of guy who would talk to Marius [another Anne Rice character].' I just left.

"For as many people who come up to me and say, 'I know what you are—turn me,' there are as many who say, 'I know what you are and I'm going to rid the world of you.' I've been attacked several times by people who think they're Van Helsing. It's amazing what people will talk themselves into," Vlad said.

Vlad admits that he's formed Dark Theater and is going ahead with his music because "I'm taking advantage of a point in time where America is really fascinated with vampires." Dark Theater is currently based in a Chicago suburb, one that could easily be renamed Geekville, despite Vlad's claim that he's "always lived a very unusual life." What this vampire is still doing there is unclear.

Vlad was a musical prodigy, playing on various horns with a single teacher until he was thirteen. His family was happy and proud, certain he would attend the conservatory and become a classical musician. But rock and roll ruined all that. "I got into Hendrix when I was three years old," he claimed. "My interest in rock stayed down in me for a while, but one day, when I was twelve, I was walking by a music store and I saw an electric guitar and said, 'Why am I playing these horns? This is crazy. I want to play that.'

"I started playing the guitar and that was the end of my career as a classical musician. After a year, I started playing with Chicago-area heavy-metal bands, working my little ass off. I was always a hired gun. Being very young and very good, I was wanted. It was a novelty for these bands to have someone so young, with hair down to his waist, a rock child in their lineup."

Finally, Vlad felt the time was right for a vampire superband and, with fanged theater masks as his logo, he started Dark Theater. Other members of the band refer to him as a little Hitler, because he writes all the lyrics and music and does all the arranging. He does like his bass player, though, and says, "I let him just go ahead and play bass." His bass player and keyboard player know that Vlad drinks blood.

Vlad calls his music "industrial Egyptian metal." His vocals sound as if they are influenced primarily by Billy Idol. The bass player and keyboard player are quite good, the latter coaxing sounds out of her equipment that makes one expect Frank Langella to appear any minute in a cloud of mist.

The first song on his home-produced cassette is "Undead," which Vlad says is their most popular tune, and is clearly about vampires. A single, simple guitar riff is repeated throughout.

To lay down in heaven
Drink from cup so sweet
Lost immortal thirsts
Feel the dead's throbbing heat
Take and feast of my soul
Glide your hands over flesh like stone
Sip from this fount of forever
Learn realms of orgasmic unknown
To lay down in heaven
Thrusting fierce so blood will flow
Sink deeper . . . Wails of pleasure
Bodies merge with ecstasy's glow.
Tear my flesh, drink my essence
Join me in eternity's snare

Undead fuck with abandon
Night endless . . . Blood cum always shared.

He's also strongly influenced by Egyptian imagery,
as evidenced by the red ankh on the back of Dark
Theater's T-shirt and the lyrics of "Rise," the second
song on the Dark Theater EP. Here he writes of "mys-
tic bonds of sand and soil / Stone flesh untouched by
year or light / Temple tombs of eternal salvation /
Rise and save the pharaoh's grace." Most people think
"Rise" is about raising the dead, according to Vlad,
when in fact it's about pyramids and their power. The
rhythm of the song conjures up visions of Rita
Hayworth dancing wildly in a club in Havana, red
skirts and hair flying.

The lyrics of his song "Lord of the Damned" reveal
much about Vlad's image of himself as vampire and
up-and-coming rock god:

I will unimagined gifts to earth
I am the lord of life
In a world doomed to darkness
Triumphant over death
I'll lock your soul in sweet caress
Let my servants be few and secret
They shall rule the many and known
Blood is the life that moves like flame
It feeds the body and soul
Come forth, children, under the stars
Take thy communion—eternity behold
Here I receive my life
Here I receive your blood.

People sometimes think Vlad's lyrics, which are certainly dark and vampiric, are intended to be Satanic. Vlad is very much against Satanism or any form of religion, including "occult and Wicca." During one performance, "Someone yelled at me, 'Satan. Satan rules.' I said, 'Satan isn't fit to lick my balls.' Even though Satan is a fictitious character, he springs from evil loins," said the self-proclaimed reincarnation/descendant of Vlad Tepes.

As of this writing, the band is unsigned and Vlad has management problems. Much to my amazement, their manager admitted in a telephone interview that she was interested in promoting the band because she was hot for Vlad. She was also heartbroken because, the previous night, he had callously and obviously flirted with someone else while he was out with her. Vlad later told me the same story, saying he had done so to nip his manager's amorous inclinations in the bud, because he does not want to have a sexual relationship with her.

There's a serious lack of professionalism here. This manager also tells Vlad not to "gyrate." "Here I am, six hundred years old," he told me in disgust, "and my manager thinks she's my mother."

Still, rock and roll being the unpredictable business it is, perhaps Vlad will be a success in two or three years, if he's snapped up by a smart producer. The time is as right as it will ever be for a vampire rock-and-roll band. With a lot of help from people who know what they're doing, Dark Theater could be it.

CHAPTER 6

I try to keep explanations short. Their attention spans aren't very long.

—ROBERT JAMES-LEAKE

The beautiful North Yorkshire coast of England has long been the holiday destination of choice for many English vacationers—so long, in fact, that in 1890 Bram Stoker went there on holiday. His idea of a pleasant vacation meant working on a pet project that he had been researching for years, and so he began writing *Dracula,* setting much of the first third of the book in Whitby.

Stoker's book helped make Whitby a tourist destination, although it already had a lot going for it, including great attractiveness, the ruins of Whitby Abbey, and a whaling museum. Most of the holiday business is in the summer, and in nearby Scarborough, which is the oldest seaside spa in England, the management of the Crown Hotel, searching for ways to generate some business in the winter, designed the Hunt-a-Vampire Weekend. Robert James-Leake, honorary secretary of the Dracula Society in London, hosts these weekends.

Scarborough stands on the still-visible foundations of a Roman signaling station. Scarborough has two bays, North Bay and South Bay, and the crag that divides them is dominated by the battlements of a medieval castle. The town itself was founded in 1622, following the discovery of discolored, sour-tasting mineral springs which were thought to have medicinal properties. In 1660, one Dr. Wittie of Scarborough began advocating bathing in the ocean water for good health, and soon it became fashionable for men and women to skinny-dip in the frigid North Sea.

The Victorian-style Grand Hotel, built in 1867, the biggest brick building in Europe at the time, quickly became known as the best hotel in Europe. The Grand, which is now a Butlin's Holiday Centre, contains 365 bedrooms, 52 chimneys, 12 floors, and 4 turrets, representing the days, weeks, months, and seasons of the year.

In the summer, visitors can watch naval battles conducted with manned scale models of ships on a lake in Peasholm Park, or they can go to the theater, or to any of the museums emphasizing natural and local history and archaeology. Mostly, visitors swim and eat and walk, for this is a coastline that invites long, peaceful, contemplative walks. The hillsides above the beaches and below the rows of large hotels are landscaped with parks and public gardens. By South Bay, there is a cluster of arcades and other amusements, which presumably occupy the jaded children of holiday makers.

The Hunt-a-Vampire Weekend I attended took place in late November, and the wind off the North Sea was strong and frigid. Not having brought a down jacket and long underwear, I was sorry to see that a long walk was out of the question.

My room at the Crown was austere, the kind of room intended for people who don't plan to spend much time in it. It had a single bed, not a problem for Europeans, but a near straitjacket for this American, used to sprawling in a king-size bed. The plumbing was topnotch, though, complete with a shower, not that common in some older British hotels. Tea-making supplies were provided, too, complete with short-bread. I had a wonderful view of the sea, which made my wall vulnerable to the icy winds, and I had to call down for an electric heater.

A large sheet of paper with a cross drawn on it covered a full-length mirror. On my pillow rested a small wooden cross, which we were advised to always keep with us, in case Robert James-Leake called for a cross check, at which point we would all be expected to hold up our crosses. Next to the cross was a box of Hofels Original Garlic Pearles—which "contain the pure essential oil of Garlic from healthy plants"—as well as a bulb of fresh garlic.

Guests were given a schedule when they checked in, with an introductory note reading, "Dear Guest, We are concerned for your safety, and as we have had this booking thrust upon us by Dr. V. Acullaa (which we think is an anagram of Vlad Dracula), who we have not yet met, we felt that we should offer you some protection. Therefore we have placed a cross and a head of garlic in your room. We would advise you to carry them with you at all times for your own safety. We hope that you enjoy your stay, as mentioned above we have not met Dr. Acullaa but do hope we will meet him during the weekend. Remember 'THE DEAD TRAVEL FAST AND IN MANY GUISES.' "

In addition, a disclaimer was included: "Dear Guest, The Management wish to welcome you to the Crown Hotel: however, we accept no responsibility for your safety during this weekend. On no account can we be held responsible for any loss of blood, loss of sleep, or profound weakness suffered between the hours of sunrise and sunset. . . . (This also applies to increased pallor of the skin and small wounds in the neck!)

"Please sign below to confirm that you have read and understood this disclaimer.

"IN THE MIDST OF LIFE WE ARE IN DEATH."

Included with the schedule and disclaimer was a sheet announcing a caption competition, inviting guests to write a caption for a scene from *Blacula,* in which Blacula has a policeman by the throat and is both growling at him and making a *Y* in American Sign Language, although he may have intended it to be a hex sign and just got the fingers wrong. A short-story competition required writers to incorporate the following words into a story: *bloody, coach, smiled, virgin, castle, delirious, inexhaustible, betrayed, impaled, rolling-pin, sandy,* and *wedding ring*.

Also in the packet for Hunt-a-Vampire Weekenders was an answer sheet for the video quiz that was held during one of the dinners, and a vampire quiz, which was to be completed at the guest's leisure and turned into the desk by 10 A.M. on Sunday. Questions included "What is the name of Stephen King's only vampire novel? *The Family of the Vourdalak* first appeared in French in the early 1840s. Who wrote it? Who played the vampire in Murnau's 1922 movie *Nosfer-*

atu? What does Renfield eat in *Dracula*? Who bought the film rights to *Interview with the Vampire*? What is Elvira mistress of?"

Since I had arrived in early afternoon, I went downstairs to check out the Crown Hotel and have some tea. The sitting room just inside the front door is furnished with large, flowered, extremely comfortable chairs and couches, and I ordered tea and a sandwich. Being one of those rare Americans who dislike coffee, I have often been frustrated over the years in restaurants when served a single cup of tea with a bag floating in it, at best accompanied by one of those little metal pots that always spill. The English understand tea. They serve up a large pot of it, often with a second large pot of hot water. It's always very good tea.

The sitting room was the kind of room that, with enough tea, one could happily sit in for hours. Soon, however, I was greeted by a very tall man, well over seven feet tall, who turned out to be Robert James-Leake. In addition to his activities with the Dracula Society, James-Leake is an actor. His greatest claim to fame is his nonspeaking role in *Return of the Jedi,* in which he stalked about quite convincingly as Darth Vader, although he's done a lot of other work as well. Probably in his mid-thirties, James-Leake is handsome, very funny, and charming, perfectly suited to host a Hunt-a-Vampire Weekend.

The Dracula Society, based in London, is a by-invitation-only society devoted to the study and enjoyment of vampire films and books. Membership is really worthwhile only to people who live in the U.K., who can attend the meetings and film screenings. They do consulting; it was Bernard Davies, one of the founders of the Dracula Society, who found himself with

George Hamilton in Budapest talking about Bram Stoker and Dracula, as well as Highgate Cemetery and Sean Manchester. I mentioned to James-Leake that I had met Manchester.

"Oh," he said, "you'll have to tell me all about that tonight at dinner. He claims to be a descendant of Lord Byron, you know," he added over his shoulder as he exited, off to decorate the dining room with skulls and bats. "Ha. Ha. Ha."

At eight o'clock, I went downstairs for the Bloody Cocktail Party in the Imperial Suite. Pitchers of Bloody Marys were waiting, as well as some plain orange juice. Post-it notes with various names on them were put onto our backs as we entered the Imperial Suite, a get-to-know-each-other device. By asking questions we were supposed to guess whose name we had. I played the game with James-Leake.

"Am I male or female?" I was male.

"Am I real or imaginary?" I was real.

"Am I good or bad?" James-Leake gave it away with his reply: "You're considered good by many people in your own country, but bad outside of it."

I was Vlad the Impaler.

Most of the people at the weekend, perhaps thirty-five altogether, had come in groups. A group of couples were hard-fisted drinkers—not so much that they became rowdy or offensive, but their idea of a good time included plenty of beer. Another group of single women had been on previous Hunt-a-Vampire Weekends; in fact, there were quite a few repeaters. Carole Gill was alone and we quickly gravitated toward each other. Her husband, with whom she owns a sweets shop in Leeds, had to stay and work at the shop.

Along with Carole, Paul Barrett and his son, ten-year-old Lincoln, proved to be my other informal companions for the weekend. Young Lincoln's intelligence and good behavior were delightful, and it was equally delightful to watch the relationship he had with his father. They shared a strong interest in horror and vampire films, and this weekend gave them a chance to spend time together. This was parenting as it should be.

Barrett is quite an interesting guy. Once a musician, he actually played in a band, Earl Fuggle and the Electric Poets, that Pink Floyd opened for back in the early seventies. Barrett had a fascinated listener as he told me about his days in the early British rock scene. He'd crossed paths with bands I greatly admire, such as Led Zeppelin and Pink Floyd. Now, completely devoted to music of the fifties and sixties, he makes a good living booking such bands around the British Isles. One of his bands, Crazy Cavan and the Rhythm Rockers, was previously named Count Dracula and the Vampires.

I was starting to relax. These were nice, normal people, probably not a blood drinker among them. No moralistic lectures were forthcoming, no intense spilling of dark, bloody secrets, at least not this weekend. And these people knew their vampire books and films. During various quizzes, I was impressed by how many people shot their hands in the air to answer the most obscure and esoteric of questions. Young Lincoln won a point for his table when he hummed the theme from *The Munsters,* quickly joined by everybody else in the room. The Munsters are very big in the U.K.

The dining room was marvelously decorated with spiderwebs, hanging bats, black candles in candelabras, skulls and rubber rats on the table, and a set of plastic fangs by each plate. James-Leake had tacked up posters from vampire movies around the room, either from his personal collection or that of the British Dracula Society, as well as a stand-up cardboard coffin promoting the movie *My Best Friend Is a Vampire!* Someone in an impressive Nosferatu mask stood on the steps and puffed atmospheric smoke into the room with either a dry ice or chemical smoke machine, like those used in horror films and rock concerts.

James-Leake pounded on the table with a heavy, gold-painted metal stake, his method of gaining the attention of the guests throughout the weekend. He explained the cross check, when he would call for all of us to hold up our wooden crosses, and outlined plans for the weekend. At his right was Julia Kruk, the new honorary treasurer of the Dracula Society, who has a day job she enjoys, as a children's librarian. Robert and Julia were amazed to learn that the "Live from Transylvania" special had been a flop. "Bernard seemed so happy," they told me. Apparently, Bernard didn't know it had been a flop, either. James-Leake rightly wrote off on the spot the consulting fee he had been expecting to receive.

They were vastly amused by my story of meeting Sean Manchester, especially when I recounted his telling me I would be able to recognize him because he looked just like Lord Byron. The Dracula Society unofficially frowns on the publicity-seeking activities of Sean Manchester. Manchester, in turn, frowns on the Hunt-a-Vampire Weekends, having said in an article in the British magazine *City Limits,* "These members of the Dracula Society who dress up at their weekends in Scarborough are analogous with those people who dress themselves up as Nazis."

The Crown feeds its vampire-hunting guests very well. The welcome dinner consisted of an attempt at Rumanian dishes, which were quite good. The appetizer of Czipetke, or a pear with walnuts and smoked salmon, was followed by Esterhazy Rostelyos, or entrecôte steak with sautéed vegetables, four different ones, all fresh and firm, as is the healthy tradition in Europe. Dessert was Szirke Gulyas Szegedi Modra, an almond and plum flan.

It was during dessert that James-Leake announced that there seemed to be a problem with several of the rooms, and asked the guests staying in those rooms to return to them and check to make sure everything was all right. The three Carol(e)s—I, Carole Gill, and Carole Bohanan, editor of *The Velvet Vampyre,* a British vampire journal—went up to our rooms.

I slipped on my fangs before going, deciding to get into the spirit of the thing. Some very high-quality fangs were to be found on this weekend. James-Leake, of course, had superb theatrical fangs and so did Kruk. Carole Bohanan's fangs were dentist-made; they cost her £100, in fact. Long, perfectly matched to her other teeth, they looked completely natural and quite attractive.

Mine were quite snazzy, too, for unprofessional fangs. They were made from Friendly Plastic, small beads of plastic which, when dipped in hot water, become soft white globs that can be fitted over one's eyeteeth, then formed into perfect, pointed fangs. They harden to the shape of your actual teeth, so that they can be popped easily back on. They come off fairly easily, too, so it's hard to chat when wearing them. Still, they look great, and an enormous tub of Friendly Plastic, enough for dozens of pairs of fangs, costs only five dollars.

We went to Carole Gill's room first. It was full of smoke from the smoke machine. As we entered the room and switched on the light, Nosferatu emerged from the smoke. Carole went screaming from the room, but I yielded to a theatrical impulse and hissed at him, showing him my Friendly Plastic fangs. When he started to come after me, though, I shrieked and ran down the hall after Carole. I couldn't quite believe myself, running around a hotel in Scarborough shrieking. I had to admit, I was having fun. I knew that the Hunt-a-Vampire crowd had been exiled to one wing of the hotel and that we were unlikely to disturb anybody.

I returned to my table and James-Leake asked me if everything was all right. "Oh, fine, no problem," I replied, smiling and giving him a glimpse of my fangs. I was delighted with his little jump and "Oooh!" although he quickly followed up with, "But it's supposed to take three days to be turned into a vampire!"

The VCR was turned on and vampire movies were shown, beginning with *In Search of Dracula*, a forty-five-minute documentary narrated by Christopher Lee and based on the fieldwork of Drs. Raymond McNally and Radu Florescu when they tracked down the ruined castle of Vlad Tepes. I'd never seen the documentary and wished to, but instead took the opportunity of talking with Carole Bohanan about her journal. Carole is a blonde, beautiful Englishwoman who enjoys dressing in stunning Victorian clothes, and she wears high-necked, tight-bodiced dresses, whether in purple, crushed velvet, or off-white cotton, very well.

Her fascination is largely with literary and film vampires, although, as the editor of *The Velvet Vampyre,* she has received letters from a few who claim to be the real thing.

Paul and Lincoln Barrett then joined me. Paul urged me to include a chapter on rock and roll and vampires in this book, and was delighted to learn I planned to do so. He told me about the song "Dinner with Drac," by John Zachalee, which was in the American Top 20 in 1958 and was then released in London, only to be banned in England by the BBC because of the lyrics, which seems ridiculous now. He sent me a tape of the song, along with some of his other favorite oldies. A passage from the song runs, "A dinner was served for three / at Dracula's house by the sea. / The hors d'oeuvres were fine, but I choked on my wine / when I learned that the main course was me."

The movies went on for some time and Horlicks, the British equivalent of Ovaltine, was served to those who thought they might need help sleeping. I should have had some, since I didn't sleep well. No matter how sensible I tried to be, I was so spooked by the man in the Nosferatu costume that I actually looked under my bed before getting into it. Dracula himself has never really frightened me, but vampires in monster form can get under my psychic skin. This Nosferatu reminded me of the one in the film version of Stephen King's *Salem's Lot,* and I have rarely been so frightened by a monster in a film.

The next morning, no doubt as part of the whole joke, my phone rang and, when I answered it, there was nobody there. The Crown continued feeding its Vampire Hunters amply and with great quality, this time with an enormous breakfast spread of fruits, cereals, and pastries, as well as taking orders for eggs, bacon (which looks like our ham), sausage, toast, and other hot breakfast food.

A bus took us through the North Yorkshire moors and Forge Valley to Whitby. Ever searching for a vampire connection, James-Leake told us you can smell garlic growing in the summer. Whitby itself sits on the steep banks of the estuary of the River Esk. The beautiful little town hasn't changed much since Bram Stoker began writing *Dracula* here, although Stoker's book has brought many tourists.

Most of those who had been on Hunt-a-Vampire Weekends before decided to skip James-Leake's walking tour and wandered off for parts unknown. He took us along the main street by the shore, pointing out along the way number 6 Royal Crescent, where Stoker stayed while he was writing the book that would lead to an industry of many more books and films, even though Stoker himself died a pauper.

Walking around the Crescent, James-Leake pointed out the guesthouse he thought Stoker might have had in mind when he described Lucy's house. Turning to me, he said, "I try to keep explanations short. Their attention spans aren't very long." Indeed, a private tour with James-Leake or Bernard Davies, who is extremely knowledgeable about Bram Stoker, would probably have resulted in a wealth of fascinating detail —but it would have taken several hours.

He pointed up the hill to St. Mary's Church, behind which sat the ruins of Whitby Abbey. Near the edge of the graveyard is a bench where both Lucy and Mina enjoyed sitting, even though an old-timer told them the bench was over the grave of a suicide. It is to this bench that Lucy goes when she is thought to be sleepwalking, climbing the 199 gently sloping steps to meet Dracula, whom Mina eventually sees bent over Lucy's figure lying on that bench. The sun reflected in the windows of St. Mary's Church inspired Stoker to give Dracula his red, glowing eyes, which Mina saw as the figure looked up when she called Lucy's name.

The names of actual persons buried in the graveyard around St. Mary's Church appear in *Dracula,* giving them an offbeat sort of immortality, including Edward Spencelagh, Andrew Woodhouse, John Paxton, John Rowlings, and Braithwaite Lowrey. Anne, the least famous of the Brontë sisters, is also buried in the churchyard of St. Mary's. The vicar of St. Mary's is still asked, much to his annoyance, "Where's that fellow Dracula buried?"

We, however, had an appointment at the Dracula Experience. This place is extremely tacky and a great deal of fun. It consists of a number of exhibits that are scenes from *Dracula,* including a shipwreck, Renfield in jail, Lucy in a coffin with a stake in her heart, a large head of Dracula, and the count himself hovering over a girl in a white nightgown. All the girls in the Dracula Experience exhibits are wearing white nightgowns. As one approaches an exhibit, one trips an infrared beam, activating the exhibit, all of which are introduced with the shrill, screaming music from *Psycho.* Doors may open to a giant bat. The shipwreck scene shows a sailor hanging on to the wheel of the ship, which moves back and forth. Sometimes strobe lights are added for effect.

In the last exhibit, Dracula is supposed to rise up out of his coffin, but the mechanism wasn't working and it greatly reduced the effectiveness of the experience to watch the owner raise the dummy count to a

sitting position so that she could fiddle with the appa-
ratus underneath. It was the end of the season, after
all; things would be all oiled and spiffed up for next
year. The Dracula Experience also displays one of the
capes worn by Christopher Lee during his tenure as
Dracula.

Then, slowly, we climbed the 199 steps that Lucy
had climbed in her nightgown to meet her fate. Carole
Bohanan, in her Victorian outfit, looked as if she was
in a time warp as she sat on one of the old, blackened
gravestones in St. Mary's Cemetery, a living scene
dragged up the steps from the Dracula Experience.

The Whitby Abbey is in ruins, thanks to the hostile
attentions of the Danes, Vikings, Henry VIII, and,
James-Leake told us indignantly, the Germans, who
during World War II shelled the ruins during an attack on the coast guard station. They're still haunt-
ingly beautiful, though, given their hilltop, seaside
setting, and, indeed, a white lady is said to haunt
them, appearing in a window from time to time.

Our bus took us back to Scarborough, where the
Crown gave us tea, after which we would have time to
put together our costumes. Some people had come
unprepared, and a costume store in the town had
brought a rackful of capes and gowns, makeup, and
masks for rent. I planned only to appear as a fancy
vampiress in black silk and rhinestones. As far as
makeup was concerned, I'd bought some mascara for
the occasion. I would wear high heels, too, even
though I can't walk in them very well.

The costumes ranged from amateurish but good-
natured (with white makeup and blood dripping down
the sides of people's chins) to elaborate and well
made. My personal favorite was Medusa, who made a

wonderful snake's-head cap for herself, but the winners were the two Ghostbusters, who had put in a lot of time on their costumes. Paul Barrett had a smashing cape and Lincoln looked effectively vampiric in his white makeup and fangs. Carole Bohanan was a vampiress, of course, in a white gown so beautiful it could have been a wedding dress. Naturally Robert James-Leake, all seven-plus feet of him, was a magnificent Dracula. He and Julia moved slowly around the dining room, from table to table, befanged Julia hissing, while Robert spoke mysteriously and quite convincingly of the dangers of midnight.

More quizzes followed, including a photo quiz which was on the back of our menu for the evening, and a quiz identifying movies, scenes from which were shown on the VCR. Next was a treasure hunt with clues left throughout the hotel, but someone in an early group stole one of the clues, so the hunt was a bust for most. The rest of the evening was devoted to dancing. Everybody was obviously having a great time.

The final morning of the Hunt-a-Vampire Weekend, after another elaborate breakfast at the Crown, was devoted to a coach tour of Scarborough. Originally it was supposed to include visits to some of Scarborough's haunted sites and Scarborough castle, but it was late in the season and most places were locked up. The driver of the coach told us of various points of interest, including the TV station and a church where he said the vicar fed the vampire bats. The vicar may very well feed the bats in his church, since they are actually lovely creatures that should be encouraged to stay around for their insect-eating abilities alone, but his bats most certainly were not vampire bats, found no further north than the Southwest United States, and mostly in Central and South America and Mexico.

Back at the hotel, we had a final substantial, excellent lunch. Most of the weekenders had trains to catch, Paul and Lincoln to Wales, Carole Gill to Leeds, me back to London. Between the talent and charm of Robert James-Leake and Julia Kruk, and the solid organization of the Crown, the weekend had gone very well. There were no disappointed grumblers complaining about not getting their money's worth, and there may very well be more repeaters next year.

CHAPTER 7

*I honestly believed that ordinary bullets would not hit her.
I thought she'd be able to dodge them. So I painted them
gold. I drank about ten cups of coffee at a doughnut shop.
I went in there, pulled [the gun] out of my pocket, and
gave her four right in the heart.*

—GABRIEL

Sometimes an obsession with
vampires and blood drinking turns violent, and even
leads to murder. That was the case with Gabriel, the
child of an otherwise ordinary family in the Pacific
Northwest, who, at the age of twenty-two, shot and
killed his grandmother with gold-painted bullets. According to court papers, he tried to drink her blood
from the bullet holes, but "she was all old and dried
up and I kept telling the voices all day I couldn't do it."
He then poured Drygas, a gas-line antifreeze made up
of various alcohols, on her body and set it on fire.

Gabriel murdered his grandmother because he believed that she was trying to poison him and also because he believed she, too, was a vampire, drinking

his blood, taking it in his sleep. Almost everybody was a vampire, Gabriel thought, and he heard voices that told him he had to kill somebody in order to get all the other vampires to leave him alone and stop drinking his blood. He believed that the vampires would throw a party for him as a reward for a successful murder and that if he killed everybody who treated him badly, he would come back as a handsome man and have a car and girls and his life would be fine.

The murder was the culmination of a life of tragedy and mental illness. Gabriel's mother testified at length at his trial, and told of the first clue his family had that Gabriel was not a normal child. Gabriel's father had taken a quarter out of his four-year-old son's piggy bank and replaced it with two dimes and a nickel. Gabriel, not understanding the value of money, became furious and called the local police, demanding that they come and arrest his father. When they declined, the boy created a booby trap with hammer and string over the door to his bedroom, so that when his father opened the door, the hammer would fall and hit him on the head.

When little Gabriel was five, he was hospitalized with pneumonia. While recuperating, he drew dozens of pictures of bare bottoms with red holes in them oozing blood. He also drew cartoons of hypodermic needles dripping puddles of blood.

His artistic depiction of his obsessions continued, and when he was in kindergarten and first grade he drew pictures of goblins, bats, witches, and scenes of violence, with shooting guns and cannons, bullets hitting people, people dying. In fact, his art teacher came to visit his parents because she was so disturbed by one particular picture, a drawing of ships with firing cannons, with extremely, frighteningly detailed pictures of the dead.

By the time he was thirteen, he had become fascinated with vampires and started drawing the mythical creatures hovering over blond-haired women with puncture wounds in their necks, blood dripping from those wounds, as well as daggers with blood dripping from them.

Around this time he started eating things that had a blood-like consistency. His mother eventually testified at his trial that he would cook up concoctions on a hot plate in his bedroom with oil, ketchup, and parts of animals, including raw fish and birds, sometimes eating the birds whole. Gabriel wandered the quiet streets of his hometown at night, hunting cats and squirrels, too. He went for days without sleeping, and once disappeared for two weeks. She also testified that these evil meals caused his teeth to become very stained.

Gabriel began using drugs—smoking pot and taking acid. When he was caught stealing some flares from a rescue truck in back of the local police station, his parents, after consulting with the chief of police, committed him to a mental hospital for six months. After he got out, he still had trouble sleeping, still wandered around at night, refused to take his medication, and was very hostile at home. He was moved to his aunt's, in the hope that a change of surroundings would help.

It didn't. Gabriel became convinced that a transmitter had been placed in his head by someone from outer space who was controlling his body. He built a cardboard pyramid that he wore as a hat because he thought it would fix his brain. He also built a pyramid structure in the nearby woods so that he could sit under it to gain its healing effects. He continued seeing a psychiatrist on an outpatient basis and, on one of those visits, he told the doctor to commit him because he was going to kill his father. The psychiatrist complied.

After a stay in yet another mental hospital, Gabriel really started to scare his family. He began keeping an ax by his bedroom door. His parents put locks on their bedroom door and that of their other son, and one member of the family would stay up at night to keep an eye on Gabriel while the others slept, locked in their bedrooms. Gabriel's mother was so frightened that, after several weeks, she went to court asking that Gabriel be removed from his parents' house.

Gabriel got his own apartment, where he lived for about six months before disappearing. When his mother went to his apartment looking for him, she found it full of trash, dirt, seaweed, and parts of dead animals and fish.

Four months later, Gabriel called from Florida and told his mother that people were after him, trying to kill him. He also told her that he had met some vampires, including one who was two thousand years old and who had given him some blood. Still, he thought they were bad vampires and he wanted to get away from them. Gabriel said he couldn't get away and was afraid, abruptly hanging up the phone.

He finally came home, but was clearly in the grip of serious mental illness. He didn't sleep at night, wash, or take care of himself. His mother was horrified to find containers in his room of what appeared to be human excrement and other containers of what appeared to be oil, blood, and parts of animals mixed together. She found him a room in a rooming house, but after only a few days, she got a call from the man who ran the place. The walls of Gabriel's room were covered with knife marks. The words SON OF SAM had been burned into the ceiling. There was dirt and filth everywhere.

In the closet was a dead cat, with the head cut off and the brain removed. Gabriel had strangled the cat with a shoestring, believing that he could resuscitate it. He said that he had removed the cat's brain to look at it and see if he could figure out how to fix his own brain, because he knew that something was wrong with his brain and had been for a long time. Gabriel also admitted that he had drunk the cat's blood. He was committed again and eventually released into the custody of his father. By this time, his parents had gotten a divorce.

Sometime during this descent into delusion and mental illness, Gabriel also hit a horse on the head with a fence post, taking a cup of blood with a hypodermic needle. When the blood got too thick to drink, he mixed it with crackers and ate it.

Shortly after he was released into his father's custody, Gabriel shot his grandmother. The testimony of the many psychiatrists who evaluated Gabriel reveals much about his state of mind before he committed the murder. He told one psychiatrist that he felt he had been mentally ill for some time and that for several years he had been hearing male voices telling him to watch out for other people who might be vampires. The voices accused and ridiculed him, telling him he was not a good person because he had not killed anyone yet. Gabriel said he thought at one time that it might have been God speaking to him, although he wasn't sure. The voices told him that if he wanted to become a vampire like everyone else, he had to drink blood.

Gabriel wanted to be like everyone else. He felt like an outcast because everyone else, he believed, was a vampire. He thought people from the group he was trying to join were stealing blood from his body at night. That included his grandmother. He believed that she used an ice pick to draw blood from his body at night while he was sleeping. Even though the psychiatrist pointed out to Gabriel that his grandmother was an invalid in a wheelchair, Gabriel said he didn't believe that and he felt that she took blood from him whenever she wanted to, because she needed it to prolong her life.

He became convinced that his grandmother was poisoning his food. It was then he decided that he had to do something to keep her from taking his blood and eventually killing him. The voices confirmed that only by killing could he become a vampire.

On the morning of the murder, Gabriel, who was living with his granduncle while looking for a job, was driven to his father's place of employment. There he picked up his father's car, supposedly to go job hunting. He went to his grandmother's house, parked around the corner, and entered by a side door.

According to the court records, his grandmother was lying on the couch when Gabriel arrived. Seeing him, she asked him to do some laundry for her. It was while he was in the basement doing the laundry that he picked up the gold-painted bullets and a gun, and brought them upstairs. His grandmother saw the gun, started yelling, and threw a glass at him. He shot her, four bullets in the heart. Although he was also accused of stabbing her and hitting her on the head, Gabriel denied that, and still does. He dragged the body off the sofa and into a bedroom, where he poured Drygas on it and set it and the bedroom on fire.

He later told his mother that the voice told him he was going to die that day if he didn't kill his grandmother. He said he fought with the voice all day and that he didn't want it to happen. He considered killing himself, but the voice talked him out of it. The bullets had to be gold, he said, in order to find their mark. He told his mother that he did drink his grandmother's blood after the murder. At other times he denied it.

He then went to an auto parts store, picked up his father, and finally returned to his grandmother's house. The fire department had arrived by then. Gabriel wanted to go into the house to pick up a gray box which had his tax returns in it, and was told that the police had it. He went to the police station and asked for the box, saying that he was going to "split town in five minutes," and that he wanted the box immediately. He was told he'd have to see a detective who wasn't there and that he'd have to come back. Gabriel made a scene, but left the police station. He was followed and seen trying to get into the rear door of the station, where he was confronted and told to leave. Gabriel hit the police officer. He was finally subdued with the help of another officer and booked for assault and battery. The next day, Gabriel confessed to the murder.

The details of Gabriel's elaborate delusional belief system, as learned in various extensive psychiatric examinations, are fascinating and deeply disturbing. Gabriel's attorney filed a plea of not guilty by reason of insanity and put psychiatrists on the stand who confirmed that Gabriel was insane and not responsible for his actions. The psychiatrists testified that Gabriel knew the difference between right and wrong, but lacked the ability to resist the impulse that caused him to shoot his grandmother. Because he was a paranoid schizophrenic, they testified he could not conform his conduct to the requirements of the law.

The prosecution wanted a murder conviction and put their own psychiatrists on the stand to counter the diagnosis of paranoid schizophrenia, suggesting instead that Gabriel had borderline personality disorder, knew the difference between right and wrong, and was capable of controlling himself. According to Gabriel's attorney, the jury was so horrified by what they heard about Gabriel's behavior over the years, particularly by his mother's testimony, that they were unwilling to find Gabriel not guilty by reason of insanity. Instead, they returned with a verdict of guilty of second-degree murder. He feels that they didn't want Gabriel on the streets again and were concerned that he might be released from a psychiatric facility much sooner than from prison.

Gabriel got life, as well as a concurrent nineteen- to twenty-year term on the arson indictment. He must serve fifteen years of his life sentence before he is eligible for parole. The parole board will be unhappy to learn of the harassing letters he's been writing to his mother. An appeal has failed. At this writing, he has served ten years.

Four psychiatrists appeared in court for the defense. Their testimony was deeply shocking. Although Gabriel didn't regard being a vampire as a crime, he was afraid other people would think there was something wrong with his mind and put him back into the mental hospital, something he very much wanted to avoid, since he'd been drugged into a catatonic state, and doctors and nurses really had taken blood from his body. He wasn't afraid of the police, though, because he believed they were also vampires and would have no reason to put him in jail. He claimed that his brain was altered by human hands and wanted doctors to fix it. He also believed that he could broadcast his thoughts.

Gabriel told one of the psychiatrists that the first time he heard a voice, it was the voice of God. Gabriel had been chopping down a tree when he heard, "Thou shall not cut down maple trees." Gabriel believed that most white people are vampires because they drink human blood, and that African-Americans are not vampires and that's why they are black. He told a doctor that a friend of his, who had blue eyes and blond hair and was well built, had claimed to be a vampire; since Gabriel wanted to be blue-eyed, blond-haired, and well built, he believed that he had to consume human blood, too.

One psychiatrist reported that Gabriel admitted to having planned to kill a friend of his, Jerry, because he believed Jerry was going to kill him. Gabriel planned to impale his friend on a pointed stick which he had already prepared and hidden in a nearby marsh, and then drink his blood. In fact, Gabriel had once punched Jerry in the nose while they were sitting at a kitchen table. When Jerry left, Gabriel tried to lick the blood off the table, but it wasn't quite enough. It was then that he went after the horse.

Gabriel told the doctors about other attempted murders as well. The first time he ever tried to kill somebody was when a friend, thrown out of his house by his parents, came to stay with him. One night, as his friend slept, Gabriel tried to shoot him with a spear gun. He'd practiced on a horse and a dog, he claimed, and believed that the spear would only bounce off his friend. Gabriel hoped to stun him just long enough to get some blood, but ultimately he wasn't able to shoot the spear.

While living in Florida, Gabriel stole a rifle with the intention of shooting somebody so he could drink his victim's blood. He took his victim to an isolated spot, but could not work up the courage to fire the shot. In another, similar incident, Gabriel picked out a victim in an isolated phone booth, but could not bring himself to shoot the man.

Gabriel also told of an incident when he was picked up, while hitchhiking, by a gay man. When the man wanted to stop at a rest area, Gabriel agreed, but before any sex could take place, Gabriel sprayed Mace in the man's face, hoping to disable him long enough to get some blood with a syringe he was carrying. The man was able to get out of the car and Gabriel got no blood.

In all these cases, Gabriel claims he didn't want to kill anybody. He just wanted blood. He told a psychiatrist that once he thought he would try to get blood from a drunk asleep on a beach by throwing a dart at him, which would paralyze him, just long enough to get the blood. He had no real idea what such actions could mean, telling of another plan he had to push an ice pick into somebody to get blood, saying he didn't think that would kill anybody. When told it probably would, he said he didn't want to kill anyone.

When I went to see him, Gabriel had been incarcerated for nine years. Much of that time had been in a maximum-security psychiatric facility, where he had received therapy, but he had recently been transferred to a medium-security prison. As I drove up, I saw the expected guard tower in the center, no doubt manned by guards with high-powered rifles, surrounded by high beige walls, topped with four rows of barbed wire.

To get to this man, who has asked that I not use his real name to protect a niece and nephew, I had to lock up my purse and all other possessions in a locker, including the cigarettes that I claimed were mine but I had actually brought for Gabriel. Apparently, visitors have slipped needles into cigarettes, small enough so the metal detector doesn't pick them up, and the only way to check the cigarettes is to break them, ruining them. I was told I could buy cigarettes in a machine inside. I hadn't brought a plastic bag, though, and so had no acceptable way of carrying change. Gabriel anticipated this and brought cigarettes of his own.

As a journalist, I was being given special treatment. The families and friends of inmates had to wait in line and fill out a form, and, if there were too many people in the visiting room, sit on hard wooden benches waiting for a few people to leave, sometimes for hours. An intimidating collection of sharpshooting medals won by prison guards was displayed in a large frame on the wall. The metal door that led to the prison was labeled DO NOT TOUCH THIS DOOR, but children who were running and playing banged into the forbidden door with no ill effect.

After passing through this first door, and having my hand stamped with ink that shows up under a special light, I had to remove my shoes and pass through a metal detector, while the canvas bag containing my tape recorder, tapes, notepad, and pen, which I had been given advance permission to bring in, was searched. I then put my shoes back on, which was one of the many dress-code requirements for entering this prison. Fortunately, it being the dead of winter, I had not worn a halter top. Nor had I worn sweatpants, a leotard, any see-through clothing, or anything that resembled the clothing of the inmates, all of which were listed as forbidden on a large wooden sign. In fact, I had gone to great trouble to be discreetly covered from neck to toe. Then I stood waiting, something Jean Harris says takes up large amounts of the time of a prisoner, first for the lock to be released on one large metal door, then another. A quick walk through the outdoors and I was at the Visitor's Center.

Except for the presence of a few uniformed guards, this visiting room looked like it could be in a hospital or even a community center. With a few exceptions, such as a heavily tattooed man with long red hair, who could have come right from central casting to play a prisoner in a Sylvester Stallone movie, these people looked like everyday, ordinary people. Children ran around laughing and playing and outside was a colorful set of blocks large enough for them to climb through. A father and a mother stood by the blocks supervising their kids. Groups of people sat around on blue or green plastic chairs—a couple here, a family group there. A priest talked with several people.

I set up my tape recorder in Lawyer's Room #1 and waited for Gabriel to arrive. Although I was watching for him, I didn't see him coming. Somehow, he just appeared at the door. Clean and neat, he had longish, straight black hair and was surprisingly handsome, for someone who didn't seem to like his looks and had said that he wanted to be blond, blue-eyed, and well built. He wore a tight black polo shirt, black jeans, and black high-top shoes. After we shook hands, Gabriel sat easily in the hard wooden chair, moving very little throughout the interview. Weighing about 180 pounds, Gabriel had no excess fat on his body, and he said he worked out a little, but that he didn't have much time for it, between working in the prison printing shop for $1.50 a day and being a jailhouse lawyer for himself and other inmates. He denied any great brief-writing ability (even though one of his lawyers praised him highly), saying there were other jailhouse lawyers in the prison who left him in the dust.

He avoided looking at me most of the time, and his eyelashes fluttered frequently as he spoke, presumably as a result of his medication. When he did look at me with his intense brown eyes, I felt distinctly uncomfortable, not because I felt physically afraid, but because I was afraid he would know that I didn't believe much of what he was telling me. Gabriel's voice was loud and firm, strongly regionally accented, and he seemed to have planned what he had to say. His attorneys had warned me that Gabriel was likely to see me only if he thought it would be in his interest. He saw me because he was lonely.

"Where do we start?" he said, taking charge of the interview for the moment.

I would say we start off by saying that I drank human blood for about ten years. I stopped about five years ago. I got more of it once I got arrested than when I was out there. It was a lot easier to get. People sort of liked giving it to me. I didn't have to fight for it. When I was on the streets, I had to beat people up and make them bleed. In prison, well, they knew that I was a vampire and so they were giving it to me.

I stopped drinking it about five years ago. It wasn't because of the AIDS epidemic, although that helped reinforce it. I've had a few AIDS tests done and they've been negative, so I guess I'm lucky, because I was drinking some of the blood from guys who were shooting heroin. I got about eighty different people, most of them, I would say, while I was in prison. I got quite a few out there, but I only killed one.

There are a lot of different reasons why I would never go back to drinking blood. There's a serious problem I had when I was consuming human blood. When your body gets accustomed to metabolizing human tissue and you don't get it, you start metabolizing your own muscle tissue. I kept losing weight and losing weight and I spent a large portion of my sentence at about 145 pounds.

Whatever the reason for Gabriel's weight loss, it wasn't because he was drinking blood, unless he was trying to live only on blood. Medical experts say the human body doesn't metabolize blood; in fact, it passes through the body without any effect unless it happens to be a very large amount of blood full of a very large amount of alcohol or drugs. Gabriel also believes that eating pork has the same effect. He says that the DNA of pigs is so close to human DNA that eating it will cause you to start metabolizing your own tissue, leaving you senile at an early age, sick and weak.

He also said he quit drinking blood for religious reasons, having noticed that all the major religions on earth forbid blood drinking, except Christianity. During Holy Communion, Christians drink the blood and eat the body of Christ. It's not just symbolic, either. Christians are taught that the process of transubstantiation is supposed to take place, where the wafer literally becomes the body of Christ and the wine or grape juice becomes the blood. Gabriel doesn't consider himself a Christian, however, although he was raised as one and does work certain Christian beliefs into his skewed, deluded morality.

I think the myth about blood drinking granting eternal life got started in the Catholic church. It was a pagan belief, but then it was adopted by high-ranking Roman governors and the early popes and it just got blown out of proportion. I would say that there are millions of people, just in this country alone, who believe that if they drink the blood of Jesus and eat his body that they're going to have eternal life.

Then there are those who take it further and say, "Well, I'm just going to take all the blood I want." I would never do it again, I'll tell you that. I didn't like losing all my muscle tone, and it took me a while to get up some tone and a build again, a manly-looking build. I think it has a physiological effect on the brain chemistry, too. It really screwed me up. I'm sure it produces a kind of madness. It's very habit-forming, because I remember when I stopped, I had a real hard time stopping. I had gut cramps and surges and all kinds of stuff like that.

When I first started drinking blood, I got a little bit of a high off it, but, after a while, it didn't do anything for me except get me all screwed up. I had the mistaken belief that it regenerates cellular tissue and probably reverses the aging process and things like that. It's a crock of shit. It doesn't. I tried it out. I gave it the acid test. It doesn't do anything.

I asked Gabriel how he got started drinking blood. He told a long, bizarre tale of cruelties his mother supposedly inflicted on him from early childhood. When Gabriel was arrested for his grandmother's murder, his mother spoke with the police and agreed to help them build a case against Gabriel by going to visit him in jail and asking him questions about the murder and his vampirism. She wanted to see her desperately ill son in an institution where he would be treated, but remembering the ax Gabriel had kept by his bedroom door and the night vigils that his family endured, she also wanted to make sure that he did not go free, at least not anytime soon.

Gabriel has sat with this knowledge for many years and has nurtured a bitter hatred for his mother. And, it seems, he has replaced his delusions about vampires with delusions about what led him to where he is now. He admits to wanting to kill his mother but says that he wouldn't because, since he's told so many people he wants to, he would get caught. He writes her letters from time to time, "telling her she's a pig, telling her she's going to hell. I like to rattle her cage, do things to try to upset her and make her paranoid and get her all upset." He says that when he gets out he will reveal the truth about his childhood, with the help of the media. He envisions an outraged mob storming her house and killing her.

Gabriel admits that his younger brother was not mistreated, and it's important to remember that this man was judged insane by several psychiatrists.

Gabriel says he was unaware of the alleged horrors of his childhood until he reached his teens. "I started to remember this later on, when I was fourteen or fifteen, and I started talking about it. Then my mother hired a doctor to do a lobotomy on me. I had a skull X ray and the radiologist says that I've had a lobotomy. Apparently my front lobes had been cut, and a piece of my right hemisphere. I don't remember the operation, but it must have occurred around the time I was fifteen. That's the time when I developed all of my serious mental problems."

Gabriel referred to his lobotomy repeatedly throughout our interview, commenting that if it hadn't been for the lobotomy, none of this would have happened. I asked him if he had a scar and he said that he had a scar under his hair, pointing to the right side of his head several inches above his ear. He said the doctors had operated on his frontal lobes too, and I commented that there was no scar on his forehead.

"There isn't?" he asked.

"No," I replied, and he changed the subject.

In fact, modern-day lobotomies are done through a patient's eye. According to a psychiatrist I spoke with, it is highly unlikely that a lobotomy would have been performed on someone as young as fifteen. And, the source added, it's not very likely that Gabriel would have had a lobotomy and not be able to remember it.

"Later on in my teens," he continued,

I started developing delusions and fears about people. I thought they were all vampires. I was very afraid. I was arming myself. I had all kinds of guns and weapons. At first I thought, well, there are only a few vampires I have to kill, and I had some wooden stakes. But then I thought, "No, that's silly. It's not going to work." A sharpened stick is not a very good weapon. So I started getting guns and knives and various things together.

I kept getting more and more paranoid. By this time, I'd been in nuthouses a few times and my brother, who was just born an idiot, because of sibling rivalry decided to team up with my mother. They decided they would get me out of the house and into an institution for life. I think they even went as far as to put tape recordings in the attic over my room to screw with my mind. I actually did hear voices later on, had auditory hallucinations. I started to believe that everyone around me was a vampire and they were all after me. I didn't think I could beat them, because there were so many of them, so I decided to try to join them. I thought that if I joined them, they'd leave me alone, stop taking my blood. So I started with animals and things like that, eating slimy things and trying to just be as gross and nasty as I could. Then I started getting into fights with people, tricking people into getting little bits of their blood.

I'd leave things arranged on the counter or the sink so that somebody would cut themselves and leave drops of blood. I'd quick jump in and say, "I'll clean that up for you. You go get a Band-Aid," and then I'd lick up the blood. There's all kinds of ways to do it. Then there's downright making somebody bleed.

The vast majority of vampires get their blood from willing donors. I asked Gabriel if he had ever had a donor.

I can only remember one before I got to prison. I can remember one night on the beach. There was a campfire and some broken beer bottles on the sand. I was sitting with a young girl, maybe eighteen years old. She leaned back on the broken glass and cut her hand. She was drunk and she said to me, "Kiss it and make it better." I started sucking on the wound and she tried to pull it away, so I sort of growled a little bit. I kept sucking her blood, taking the blood out, pulling really hard, pushing my teeth against the skin and pulling, sucking really hard to get all the blood. I was bringing her flesh into my mouth, too, to make sure all of the blood came out.

And she said to the other people sitting around the campfire, "Hey, he's sucking my blood." Nobody paid any attention to her. So I just kept it up and kept it up until she really got mad. And when she got really mad and was getting ready to hit me, I stopped. I think there were some other donors, but I can't remember them.

Gabriel gradually led up to the subject of his grandmother's murder, speaking in a deliberate, matter-of-fact way.

At any rate, there was a lot of paranoia in me, and I was constantly thinking that I was being hunted, that people were ganging up on me and conspiring against me to poison me and to steal my blood. I was getting mad as hell about it. I had guns. I knew I was a lot stronger than a lot of these people that I thought were persecuting me. I would try to intimidate them, telling them to back off or I'd kill them, and they wouldn't listen.

I remember once I was living in a run-down flophouse, all winos, this teenage boy used to break into the room all the time, just turn the knob real hard and force the lock open. And then he'd fall asleep in my room. Naturally, I suspected that he liked to sleep in my room because he wanted to steal my blood. So one day I loaded up a flintlock. I emptied eight firecrackers into it, and put a .44-caliber ball in, and used a firecracker fuse because I didn't have a flint for it. The hammer was back on it, so that means the breech was open, so it lost compression when I fired it. If I had dropped the hammer after the fuse disappeared, it would have blown his head off, but I didn't know that. I was under the delusion at the time that bullets bounce off people and this sort of strengthened my delusion.

This boy was sound asleep in my chair and I got him one right in the forehead and he jumped up and said, "Gabriel, the room's on fire!" because eight firecrackers-full of gunpowder filled the whole room with smoke in a flash. He had powder burns all over his face, a big lump on his forehead, and his hair was smoking.

He figured out what happened and stopped sleeping in my room. He told the police a few days later and they didn't believe him. They told him, "You're smoking the same shit he is." I just wanted to render him immobile so I could get some of his blood. He thought I was mad at him over the girl he was dating or something.

Shortly after that I thought that my brain had been cut open. I thought that somebody put something in there, because I was hearing voices. I thought there was a transmitter in there. So I decided to perform surgery on my own head. I decided to practice on a cat. I strangled the cat with a shoestring. I was under the impression that if I breathed into its nose and mouth, I could resuscitate it. I cut open the brain, but I made a real mess of it and the cat didn't revive, so I had this mess. I had this cat in my apartment with its brain in a glass. I took the brain out after I realized the cat was dead; I took it out to look at it. I had it in a glass and I had the cat's body on a sheet of glass that I had found.

There were a lot of people in the hallways so I couldn't get rid of it right then, so I put it in my closet, hoping that later on late at night I could bury the cat. But that teenage kid came back, and decided to break into my room. He was drunk and wanted a place to crash, so he went in there, opened up the closet, found the cat, and called the police.

I was sent to a nuthouse, where I told them

that my brain had been cut open. If they had X-rayed my skull back then and realized that I had been lobotomized, none of this would ever have happened. I didn't like it at the hospital. They put me in a locked facility and while I was there, there was an article in the newspaper saying the well had been poisoned at this hospital. The water tasted awful. It tasted like it could kill you, and they weren't giving us any distilled water. They weren't giving us anything to drink. You'd get a little cup of juice if you decided to take your medication. I didn't want the damned medication because it slowed me down, it made my heart ache. I didn't like it. I didn't trust it.

These people were trying to hurt me. So I didn't even bother talking to them about my fears. I just said, "I'm not taking it," and I escaped, because the water was poisoned. I said, "This is a deathtrap here." I got taken back by the police, escaped again. I didn't have to go back the second time. I got even. I did them good, too. I screwed up the ceiling, caused about five hundred dollars' worth of damage to the ceiling when I escaped. They were really cruel to me, so I'm not sorry about ruining their ceiling.

I went to live with my grandmother. The neighbors told me that she had pushed her second husband down the stairs. While he was alive, every time that I went over there, he was covered with cuts and bruises all over, some bleeding lesions oftentimes. He was an old man, and he was terribly gone in the head, for some reason. I'd never seen anyone quite that soft in the head before, and I've been in nuthouses. While I was there, the neighbors were telling me, "Yeah, she used to push him down the stairs," and he went into a coma and died shortly after the so-called fall down the stairs.

So I wasn't too wild about living with her, because both my real grandfather died when he was married to her, and her second husband died. And she had this sinister laugh. She was always laughing, used to drive me batty.

Gabriel stopped and smiled broadly when he made this little joke. It was clear that I was expected to respond, so I smiled and said he was very funny. A little girl pressed her face against the glass window of the attorney's room and Gabriel rapped lightly on the glass. He went on to describe the delusions and fears that led to the killing of his grandmother and even suggested that it was really a mercy killing.

"I began having auditory hallucinations," he continued. "I would imagine that I was hearing other people's thoughts. When people came close to me, I thought I was reading their mind. We all know that's impossible, don't we?"

It was a direct question, more like a challenge. I muttered something about not knowing if it was possible or not, since there has been a lot of legitimate research on telepathy, something of great interest to Gabriel, who mentioned secret research being done by the CIA at UCLA. He seemed pleased that I had not completely brushed off the possibility of telepathic thought, and returned to his narrative.

"I was getting real, real scared, and then I started smelling poison. I didn't imagine it. I've never heard of an olfactory hallucination," he said, although if he had asked his psychiatrists they would have told him that olfactory hallucinations do occur.

He went on,

So I said, "All right. I won't eat food." I lived right next to the ocean so I started grabbing things that were stuck to rocks and boiling them and eating them. The things I was eating are very expensive in restaurants, mussels, snails, any fish that I could catch, sometimes lobsters. I grabbed my own food, because I assumed that this lady was crazy, that she was out of her mind. She was trying to poison me and drink my blood.

She was dying. She had cancerous tumors all over her spine. When she died, she was in a wheelchair. Two months before, she had an operation where they severed her spine to reduce the pain, and that's what put her in the wheelchair. Before that, she could walk rather quickly. With a cane, she could walk rather quickly. She used to do it every morning, very loud, thumping back and forth, very quick, like a robot or something.

At any rate, I started smelling poison in the food and it wasn't any sophisticated poison; it smelled identical to that stuff you throw on the rosebushes. I decided that I wasn't going to be the third man to die that lived with her. So I moved in with my uncle.

But I was hearing these voices that kept saying, "If you let her get away with it, we're all going to do it to you." I kept hearing that, a couple of times a day, and it really bothered me. I was thinking like, jeez, they crucified this guy Jesus and they take his blood or something, because he forgave everybody. I should be a real mean son-ofabitch and kill a lot of people. And, you know, if I hadn't gotten arrested for killing my grand-mother, I would have killed quite a few people, anybody I suspected was bothering me.

I shifted uneasily and asked him, "And not gotten caught?"

"Yeah," he said.

But I would still be crazy. So it's sort of a trade-off. I've lost ten years of my life. Actually, my whole life's been hell on earth.

Anyway, the day that it happened, I was getting more and more psyched and hearing a lot more people. I could feel like everyone crowding in on me like they expected me to do it, because she had two weeks left to live. She even said she wanted to die. When she snapped out of the Di-laudids and the Quaaludes she was on, she said, "I don't want to live." Her spine was severed. She was in pain. She had cancer.

So I thought, "She wants me to do this. That's why she put the goddamned poison in the food. She wants me to do this. The whole town expects me to do this, to join their club, to be a vampire. You've got to kill somebody to show that you've got some savvy.

"But you've got to cover it up a little bit to make it look like everything's all right, because there are some people who aren't vampires and they'd want things to go quietly in the town and not make any waves." So I thought I had to de-stroy the body so it doesn't come back to life, anyway. I figured I'd make it look like a fire.

Fire's the best way to destroy the vampire, anyway. I'll make it look like she died in a fire.

I honestly believed that ordinary bullets would
not hit her. I thought she'd be able to dodge
them. So I painted them gold. I drank about ten
cups of coffee at a doughnut shop. I went in
there, pulled it out of my pocket, and gave her
four right in the heart.

He delivered those words "gave her four right in
the heart" with no emotion at all. He could have easily
been saying that he had given his grandmother an
apple. He seemed satisfied that he had done it. He
may even have felt proud. There didn't seem to be a
trace of remorse.

"I figured, 'This is it,' " he said. " 'Anyone that wants
to try and take my blood, I'm killing them. I'm tired of
losing my blood to all you fucking vampires!' "

The story was told. I felt drained, and would have
liked nothing better than to leave that tiny room,
make my way through all the steel doors with their DO
NOT TOUCH THIS DOOR signs, get my coat out of the locker
and drive away. I was sure that nothing I had said
would be picked up on the tape, since my voice
sounded so faint and weak to me, next to his loud
male voice. I was thirsty, too, but because I hadn't had
a plastic bag for change, I wasn't able to buy a soda
from the row of vending machines lining the entrance
to the Visitor's Center. But Gabriel had more to say.

"After I got busted and went to prison, I found out
that most people don't think that way, that I was kind
of an oddball. Sometimes a celebrity, most of the time
an oddball. I started to develop a delusion that maybe
it was a good idea to drink blood. After all, I've got a

long bid, and if I drink blood, I won't get any older. Even if they keep me until I'm fifty, I'll still be a teenager or something. So I tried to get as much blood as I could. I let a lot of people know that I wanted blood. And I started getting it all the time. There were guys who were shooting heroin who were giving it to me. There were homosexuals—the place was packed with homosexuals," he said. "But I passed both of my AIDS tests negative."

The other prisoners are spooked by Gabriel. When a new man arrives, he quickly gets word that Gabriel's a vampire. The more superstitious are soon wearing a cross around their necks. At first, some would grab it and hold it up when Gabriel would walk by them, but he told them that it didn't help anything, that it just pissed him off, so they stopped.

I asked him about overcrowding, a big problem in prisons now.

"Oh, I don't worry about that," he told me. "Nobody will room with me."

He paints, but for years lacked the money to buy materials. He recently received some canvases and paint, however, and the prison has given him a spot in the basement in which to work. He likes Tchaikovsky's *Swan Lake* and wants to do a painting of an upside-down swan with fishes dancing around.

"Kind of perverse," he said, describing the planned painting. "I enjoy painting and I do good paintings, but I think literature is a higher form of art and I'd really like to write a novel. In fact, there's a writer's workshop here tonight."

Gabriel doesn't plan to write his novel, though, until he's out of prison and has a word processor, which is forbidden in prison. He reads, too, and at the time of the interview was reading Faulkner's *Light in August*. He likes Faulkner and thought *The Sound and the Fury* was "dynamite." He was never a big fan of vampire books or movies.

As prisoners often do, Gabriel corresponds with various people.

I was corresponding with a very sick lady in California when I was still drinking blood. I think she's dead now. She said her name was Misty. I got a picture of her. She looked like death warmed over. She was wearing a black robe with a high collar and a red velvet liner, and she had long, I don't know, it looked like peroxide garbage hair. It was really gross-looking hair. She had boils all over her face and the last I heard from her, she was in the hospital for something.

She says people give her blood, that she doesn't take it from anyone. She said she also likes to take it out of pigs and chickens and all that. A bunch of nonsense. I believe her. I believe she was doing that. I personally wouldn't recommend anybody to drink blood out of a chicken or pig or any living thing, for that matter, but especially out of a pig or chicken, because you know what happens when you eat raw pig or raw chicken. And you can imagine what's floating around in that blood isn't exactly healthy, you know. It could kill you in a flash, the things that are in there, things, little tiny worms that crawl into your heart.

Gabriel asked me if I would like to know some places where vampires gather to drink blood. He told me about a swamp near Nokomis, Florida, which is next to Venice, and a shocking murder that he claims to have witnessed there.

A lot of them hang out there and have parties at night. They light a big fire out in the swamp and they do unusual things. I didn't see anyone drinking blood, although they talked a lot about it, and they murdered a teenage girl while I was there. I saw it. I didn't do it. I had a rifle right on the front seat of my car, a loaded rifle, and I didn't do anything to stop it because I was all crazy in the head, and I thought that they were sacrificing her to me or something and that it was necessary.

It was really sick. She was laughing like crazy, wouldn't stop, on the ground right next to the fire. This guy was kicking her in the chest and everything. She wouldn't stop laughing. Apparently she was drugged, because I don't know anybody that laughs when they're getting kicked like that.

So I'm there drinking this big bottle of Almaden wine along with a guy from Cleveland, Ohio, that I hooked up with down there. And we were just watching, leaning against my car, drinking, getting a little buzz on from the wine.

The guy tied her hands to the grille of the car, right, and he got in the car, put on the headlights, started the engine, and put it in reverse, dragging her. She was still laughing, right. And so everybody stopped what they were doing and somebody shut off the music. There was a big eight-track playing on somebody's car stereo.

Somebody shut it off, right. So everything's quiet and we're watching, she's there laughing, getting dragged slowly backwards.

All of a sudden, he put it in forward. There was this big loud snap like a zucchini snap, and she stopped laughing. And then someone next to me said, "Now we're all going to take her apart and eat her." And I said, "Oh, shit, I'm getting out of here."

So I got in my car. The whole time I had a loaded rifle on my seat. It was probably a runaway girl or something. She couldn't have been more than fifteen. Anyway, all the young men and women started clustering around her, and I just took that chance to make an anonymous exit from the place.

He also told me about some people in his hometown.

These people call themselves vampires, but they are just sick puppies who think that they're going to get power. See, most people start this nonsense because they're unhappy with what they are, and they think that by getting into Satan worshipping, they're going to be enhanced somehow, that they're going to be popular, they're going to get powers. I mean, you have vampires in the movies, they always have total control over their lovers. They manage to do whatever they like with impunity it seems, until the end of the movie. That seems attractive to some people, and they want it. They really believe that they're going to acquire powers which are nonexistent. They think that the devil can give them powers.

Gabriel then described his beliefs about God and Satan.

I happen to believe there's God and Satan, but I don't think there's any struggle involved. Satan would cease to exist, in my opinion, if God wanted him to. I think it's necessary for Satan to exist. Evil is necessary to keep order in the universe. Someone has got to burn in hell to keep order in the universe. I believe we're all immortal. All humans are immortal. After we die, we're reassembled someplace else, depending on what we did in this life. We've got temporary flesh to accomplish whatever righteous deeds we can accomplish while the temporary flesh holds together. And then you're judged. Everything's held on the balance.

I don't believe that anyone died for our sins. I don't think it's possible for one person to pay for the sins of another. The guy's got a good, you know, God's got a big heart. He says, "I can overlook that, I can overlook that, I can't overlook that." It's a test. If enough good is in our balance when we're judged, we go to someplace where we're happy, a life where we have everything we want. But there have to be evil people to burn in hell to keep the universe going. Their life energy has to burn to support all the universe.

I would have been better off if I was killed. I often think I'd like to punch God in the nose for not letting me die back then, the first time she tried to kill me. I'd never commit suicide. It's against God's rules. You can't commit suicide. You got to stick it out.

I asked him if he'd ever wanted to kill himself. "Oh, yeah, I've wanted to," he said. "I hate life. But I've got to stick it out and see whatever comes, fight down to the last breath."

Many people would call Gabriel evil. But as I sat there watching this man who had led a life of pure hell from early childhood, I just couldn't come to the conclusion that he was evil. Gabriel is sick. His brain isn't normal and it doesn't work the way it should.

In fact, he has good and generous impulses. When I asked him where he would be and what he would be doing if he could be anywhere he wanted, doing anything he wanted, he told me he'd buy a medium-size house, and get a boat, and spend lots of time scuba diving. He studies history and likes to dive looking for wrecks, maybe salvaging something old, possibly valuable. If he could be set for life, he went on to say, with three to five million dollars from one of his perjury lawsuits, then he would live quietly, diving, painting, and writing.

He also would attend meetings for worthy causes, such as Greenpeace and the American Society for the Prevention of Cruelty to Animals. It's possible that Gabriel feels bad about all the animals he killed, even if he doesn't feel particularly bad about his grandmother. When he had more money, he sponsored a little boy in Colombia through one of the foster parents' programs. Inmates who spoke Spanish helped Gabriel write to his foster child in Spanish.

Gabriel doesn't seem to be in touch with reality

about what his life really would be like if he did ever get out. He'd like to teach, he says, perhaps social studies or art in a high school, although he realizes that people might not like the idea of him teaching their children. He has gotten an associate's degree in business since he's been in prison and is working towards a bachelor's degree in sociology.

"I might be considered valuable as a teacher," he told me, "because of the extraordinary things that I've endured and the experiences I've had, able to counsel people, and teach them about society."

Gabriel claims that he's gotten his case reopened, having written the brief himself. He said that a judge is considering overturning his conviction because at least five people committed perjury to get him convicted and that certain corrupt members of the state government wanted to make a political statement with his case. At that time, Gabriel says, the governor wanted to take the insanity defense off the books and change it to "guilty but insane." That way, the criminal would get the same amount of time but would receive treatment.

Gabriel agreed to speak with me even though the judge in the case had told him to lay low, and one of the conditions of the interview was that I wouldn't speak to his current attorney, who did not know that Gabriel had consented to an interview. When I saw Gabriel, he expected, quite unrealistically, to be free within six months. Even if the conviction were overturned and a new trial ordered, it's unlikely that someone with his psychiatric history would be released on bond. He is taking medication which he says "stimulates the production of a hormone in my brain, so that it dampens haphazard signals." He doesn't like it and wants to stop taking it, believing that if he was in a less hostile environment, he wouldn't need it. He doesn't believe he needs to be in a hospital, either.

Being free is all Gabriel is living for. In spite of the horror of what he had done, I felt compassion for him because he is so obviously sick, and needs treatment not punishment. The psychiatric institution that Gabriel was in before he was transferred to a prison was just as bad, he says, and no doubt it was. There doesn't seem to be any place for someone like Gabriel. His life has always been hell and probably always will be. It wasn't the smallness of the interview room or the loudness of Gabriel's voice that made me feel so overwhelmed and choked, it was the utter hopelessness of his situation.

The urgent desire of Gabriel's family and the jury to keep him off the street is understandable. The things that were wrong with his brain are still wrong and always will be. He hasn't taken any responsibility for his actions, and probably isn't capable of doing so. He still retains some of his old delusions, and still believes that his grandmother was trying to poison him. His elaborate stories about his mother and the deep hatred he has for her are not coming from a mentally healthy person.

I packed up my equipment and turned to shake Gabriel's hand.

"I might be a little bit more violent than I was before I came into prison," he told me, "but I'm all right now, I think."

CHAPTER 8

It goes beyond sex. It's really one of the most intimate things you can do.

—SHANNON

Beginning with Bram Stoker's *Dracula,* a strong erotic undercurrent has been apparent in most, although not all, vampire books and films, which are the inspiration for many modern-day blood drinkers, although they often deny such influence. When Bela Lugosi came along, even though many people found him downright ugly, the visual expression of Stoker's idea of a count dressed in evening clothes and a long, flowing cape, speaking with a foreign accent which sounds sexy and sophisticated to some, was so successful that Dracula has appeared in films again and again.

With Frank Langella's Dracula, however, sex became the dominant theme. From the moment he curls his hand over Mina's when she discovers him washed ashore from a shipwreck, the sexual tension begins to build. Although not a popular success, the film is one of the most erotic vampire movies ever made (along with *The Hunger,* which stars three of the sexiest, most attractive people walking the earth, David Bowie, Catherine Deneuve, and Susan Sarandon).

In literature, too, vampires are turning up as less monster and more human, with passions and lust, not just blood lust. Anne Rice's Lestat novels are especially compelling, and Rice writes of erotic matters powerfully. Her defiant rock-and-roll vampire who breaks all the rules, vampire and human, has become a fantasy figure for many of her readers.

Shannon, a twenty-five-year-old woman for whom vampirism and sex are integrally connected, is a big fan of Anne Rice. Like many people attracted to vampires, in fiction and fact, Shannon finds modern-day life to be too shrill and bright and is drawn to the night. The romance and power of Lestat are far more appealing than the average real-life man, who, along with his everyday struggles and insecurities, these days is apt to have some underlying hostility towards women. Although Shannon doesn't live in a fantasy world, she has integrated some of the features of the vampire world into her life. This includes drinking blood.

When I met Shannon, she was dressed in blue jeans and a cream-colored sweater. She wore her hair in a punk cut and sported half a dozen pierced earrings in each ear. Unlike many punkers, whose look and world she only dabbles in anyway, Shannon does not have a scrawny, pale appearance, but was instead voluptuous and sensual.

Shannon is bright. She was eager to talk about her feelings and experiences, perhaps as a way of validating them. Being a vampire can be a very lonely business, and she was interested in knowing what other vampires were doing, too. Shannon calls herself a vampire for lack of a better term, although she was quick to say that she doesn't think she's immortal and she doesn't have fangs. Nor does she sleep in a coffin, although she does wear a cape on occasion, her concession to the dramatic.

"I think I was born the way I am," she said, "because as far back as I can remember, I always loved horror movies and stuff." A single child, Shannon comes from a liberal family. Although her mother still would call herself a Catholic, she doesn't go to church, believes in abortion and birth control, and has no problem with homosexuality. Shannon's father is an atheist and so Shannon had no real religious upbringing, instead being encouraged to think for herself, something for which she is very grateful.

She lives at home, because she can't afford a place of her own. She makes lousy money as a customer service representative in a large corporation. To qualify for a better job, Shannon is going to school two nights a week, learning computer programming. Her true love is art, especially portraiture, and she hopes to go to art school after she's saved enough money with a computer job.

She describes herself as close to her parents, although things weren't always that way. When she was sixteen, she got married, in part because she wanted to get away from her family. She says now that she was stupid. She moved to the South with her husband, but the marriage ended after a few years. She's a feminist now.

"I didn't like being married," she says. "I never realized until I was married how much control it gives someone over your life. I never want to be in a situation like that again. People say to me, 'Oh, you just had the wrong husband.' But the idea of someone having that much control over me again terrifies me."

Shannon's parents have gradually become aware that she drinks blood, although they don't really know the details. They see her books and newsletters about vampires and they see the row of thin white scars on her forearm. There are about a dozen of these slender marks, no more than an inch and a half long, together in a row perhaps four inches long, cuts made when she gave her blood to her lovers. She says her parents seem to have the attitude that "if it makes you happy, that's fine with us, dear."

Shannon is lucky. Some parents have put their vampire children in mental hospitals, even if those children were functioning well. Most people just can't accept this business of blood drinking. It's horrible and sickening to them. Shannon knows this and is very careful about sharing the details of her secret life, especially with doctors.

Shannon has a rare blood condition, which she describes as the opposite of hemophilia. Her blood clots very quickly, so quickly that after one attempt to donate blood to the Red Cross, she realized she would never be able to. She knows she inherited this condition from her mother, although she has no idea if anybody else in her family has ever had the desire to drink blood. Shannon's doctors discovered her blood condition when they were diagnosing her arthritis, also a hereditary illness. Her swollen joints, especially her fingers but also her feet, knees, and elbows, are now being successfully treated, but doctors have been unable to learn more about her blood condition, be-

cause Shannon doesn't feel like being a guinea pig,
and hasn't allowed them to test her further. She has
no symptoms as a result of this condition and generally feels fine, and since there is no treatment or cure,
she just wants to be left alone. She doesn't know if
there is any connection between her desire to drink
blood and her blood condition, although she thinks
there could be. She hasn't told the doctors about her
blood drinking, since she expected them to react
badly.

Like most vampires, Shannon says she can sense
when someone else is a vampire. By chance, one of
her coworkers is a vampire. He has a girlfriend, so
there's no involvement, but she knew right away when
she met him, and they've discussed their blood drinking.

"I started thinking about drinking blood at the
same time I started thinking about boys," she said,
"but I didn't actually do it until I was almost twenty-
two."

She was dating Tom, a man fourteen years older
than she. One night they were talking about their sexual fantasies and Shannon told him about her desire
to drink blood. Tom said that he had known another
woman who had been a blood drinker. When Shannon
asked Tom if she could drink his blood, he agreed. He
wasn't turned on by the idea, but he was willing to
experiment.

With the corner of a razor blade, Tom cut the tip of
his finger. Shannon doesn't cut or pierce her donors,
taking no conscious pleasure in their pain, however
minor. She doesn't even want to watch when they cut
themselves. She says that pierced fingers aren't a
very good source of blood and it's not her method of

choice. She usually drinks only a very small amount, anywhere from half a teaspoon to a couple of tablespoons, and it takes a while to get that much out of a pierced finger. It takes a while anyway, she says, because she doesn't like her donors to make big gashes. They don't cut deeply, in part to avoid a serious scar, and they don't cut a vein. Blood has an iron taste to Shannon and all the blood she has drunk tasted pretty much the same to her. The taste isn't important to her.

Since that first time with Tom, Shannon has drunk the blood of three other lovers. It's not something she'll do with just anyone. It's not just a question of all the dangerous, sometimes fatal, sexually transmitted diseases. Not every man is willing to experiment and many would be horrified at the idea. Most important, the act of blood drinking has to be with someone she really cares about and, usually, someone she has known for some time.

"It goes beyond sex. It's really one of the most intimate things you can do. That's why I don't drink just anybody's blood, although I know people who claim they do. It's an intimate thing. I feel as though I'm actually taking part of the person. There's no way that I know to become more intimate than that," she says.

Blood drinking is her only sexual kink. She has a leather jacket, but isn't "into leather." She's run into a few guys who wanted to spank her and she allowed them to, but thought it was "rather stupid." She describes herself as 90 percent heterosexual. Shannon's best friend, Terri, knows about Shannon's blood drinking, and teases her about it, but Terri has her own sexual kinks so Shannon just teases her back.

She and Terri have made love and it was then that
Shannon felt the desire to drink Terri's blood.

"Terri probably would have let me and wouldn't
have been horrified, but I don't think she really
wanted me to and we both would have felt odd afterwards, so I didn't," Shannon said.

When a coworker cut himself at work once, holding
up his finger which had blood running down it, Shannon did have the desire to suck his finger. Although
the coworker wasn't a close friend, she does like him,
and feels that's why she had the impulse. If the blood-
ied finger had been on the hand of someone she
doesn't like, it wouldn't have been so attractive.

Shannon has an extensive correspondence with
dozens of vampires around the country and she and
Marcia, a fellow vampire in the Midwest, exchange
lengthy letters and photographs. They've also had extended telephone conversations and are toying with
the idea of drinking each other's blood when they
eventually meet. Marcia has a hard time of it. Originally from a small town, she could find no like-minded
people. Now she's in a city, and has found a few fellow
vampires, making it possible for her to follow her vampiric instincts.

Shannon also corresponds with Sandy, a sixteen-
year-old girl who became a vampire at fifteen. Her
correspondence with Shannon is very important to
her. Whenever she mentions drinking blood to her
friends, however casually, they either don't take her
seriously or think she's "incredibly morbid."

Sandy and I have corresponded. Sandy calls herself
a "basically normal teenager although I do tend to
dwell on the dark side of life and always had a fascination with death." She feels that her fascination with

vampires goes hand-in-hand with that. She doesn't believe that there are immortal vampires with fangs who live on blood, rather defining a vampire simply as a person who drinks blood. Those people who believe they can't live without blood have a psychological need, Sandy wrote, not an actual physical one. Still, she wishes that there really were vampires, so that she could be one.

"My dream," she wrote, "would be for a gorgeous Gothic vampire from the 18th century to come into my room one night and make me immortal. Then we could live the nightlife together. I know that sounds dumb, but it's true."

When Sandy met Steven, whom she calls the "most perfect guy I've ever known," she had just been dumped by a previous boyfriend, and Steven, then eighteen, helped her get over it. They shared the same musical tastes, an important bond among teenagers, including a predilection for the Ramones, the Sex Pistols, the Misfits, the Cramps, the Dead Kennedys, Bauhaus, the Damned, Peter Murphy, Christian Death, the Sisters of Mercy, and 45 Grave. Sandy frequently dresses in black and has a lot of jewelry in the form of bats, skulls, crosses, ankhs, skeletons, spiderwebs, and handcuffs, all very punk.

Sandy and Steven shared an interest in vampires as well. Sandy told Steven that the appeal for her was the power, the romantic lifestyle, and immortality. When she asked him what the appeal was for him, he answered simply, "The blood."

Sandy continued in her letter,

> He told me about the desire he'd always had, not a burning desire, just a desire to share a plea-

surable and intimate act with someone special. "Like sex," I thought. But he said it went way beyond sex. Everyone had sex. But how many people would actually share their blood with you? Steven told me I was one of maybe three girls he'd ever been able to tell that to. It made me feel special that he could confide in me. The first time he drank my blood we were having sex and he asked if he could cut me. At first I felt uncomfortable, but it really was an incredible experience. He let me drink from him and it was magical. I felt—sometimes still do—closer to him than anyone I'd ever known. It was the most intimate experience I've ever had. Unfortunately, Steven and I were separated (mostly my fault) and never found each other again. But his memory will live with me always.

I've never done that since. I've never really loved any of the guys I know enough to tell them about it. Even though I haven't loved anyone since then, I hope to find a partner I can share this with again. Since then, I have had the craving for blood a few times. When this happens I simply cut my arm and drink my own blood. It brings back the memories, which always makes me cry.

Both Sandy and Shannon link blood drinking with sex and intimacy. Neither will drink the blood of just any lover, only someone they truly love.

Sandy says, "To me, sex is nothing. It's never meant much to me probably because it means so little to the guys who do it with me. I needed something intimate that I could share with only the guy that I love. Steven gave me that when he offered me his blood. Perhaps the taste makes me feel that way again and that is why I crave it."

It's not enough to dismiss Shannon's and Sandy's blood drinking as just another sexual variation, lumping it together with a taste for leather or rubber or S and M, or any of the other many varieties of sexual activity. Love and intimacy are hard to find in modern American life. The sexes are having trouble connecting and both want a great deal more from each other than was expected in relationships thirty years ago.

For vampires, that intimacy is even harder to find. Their hunger is satisfied only by going to the edge, with the slash of the razor blade and the flow of blood, and the act has tremendous power for them. Still, crossing the line from mere sex to true blood intimacy doesn't guarantee the success of a relationship, as both Shannon and Sandy know.

Sandy said, "I guess I like it because it makes me feel special if somebody's willing to literally give me part of their life. Because you need blood to live on, you're giving somebody part of your life if you offer them your blood. Sex is purely selfish, while blood drinking is the opposite."

She admits that she and Steven were drug users, but says they never took anything when they drank blood. "There's no drug in the world that could equal or enhance that feeling," she wrote.

Shannon also knows a group of vampires in Salem, Massachusetts, who she calls the North Shore Lost Boys. She dated Jerry, who claimed to have been born in 1567, but it ended badly and they're not in touch now. Jerry and his friends and some sixty others are part of an informal vampire network in Massachusetts.

They can be found in certain Boston clubs, such as the Rathskeller or the Channel, when certain bands are playing. The music is punk, new wave, or hard core, not heavy metal. Shannon doesn't like the devil-worship subject matter of some of the heavy metal bands. Curtain Society and Sleep Chamber are two Boston-area bands that draw the vampires out to dance. Some of their fans are rumored to practice self-mutilation. In the band Requiem in White, the lead singer dresses like Dracula. Requiem in White has as many as one hundred vampires in their crowd; other bands have perhaps forty mixed in their audiences.

Some of the dancing vampires dress like Dracula, too, including makeup and fangs, while others look like punk rockers. They all know each other, at least by sight, but small details can give them away to the nonvampire observer. Poison rings are popular among this group, rings which resemble, at first glance, class rings. But the stone lifts up, and inside is a small well, supposedly for holding poison. Shannon has a poison locket. Jewelry made of human bone or teeth is an indicator, too, and Shannon has an earring made of a human tooth.

Although one might automatically assume that these punk vampires must be doing drugs, and many of them probably are, Shannon no longer does. She doesn't even drink or smoke cigarettes. She used to use cocaine, but stopped after, as she puts it, learning the hard way.

The majority of vampires, says Shannon, are not obvious. They live fairly straight lives, dressed in whatever clothing they must wear for their day jobs. Unless, like Shannon and many other vampires, one has the antenna to sense them, it's impossible to tell a vampire from your next-door neighbor or coworker. They keep their vampirism a secret for the most part, because they're afraid that someone might try to hurt them, a common and, unfortunately, realistic fear.

Some drink animal blood, but Shannon has no such desire. When she worked at a pet shop, a kitten cut his paw and struggled while she tried to bandage it for him, splashing blood on her face and her hair. She simply washed it off. Shannon could live without drinking blood, but she's happier with it. Since it's tied in with her sex life, it's an important part of her life, something she thinks about every day. Her correspondence with other vampires around the country is important to her, too. She doesn't feel that she's doing anything sick or wrong or bad or that there's anything negative at all about what she's doing. To Shannon and to Sandy, being a vampire is an acceptable alternative lifestyle. Shannon feels that people are too quick to condemn.

"For me, it's always been an activity between two consenting adults," she says. "The same guy who'll condemn me may batter his wife or hit his kids and think it's OK for him to do that, but that it's not OK for me to drink blood."

Several psychologists who read the transcripts of my interviews, including the one with Shannon, do not agree. One said of Shannon, "She's got a neediness that the other vampires have. There's nothing inside, therefore suck on somebody's wrist to get some life blood to feel alive. I don't get the feeling that this is sexy to her as much as it is a yearning for caring, warmth, and to have something special about herself."

Another labeled Shannon a sociopath, saying that

while she is not psychotic, "her bland acceptance of what is actually a destructive impulse . . . glosses over what is destructive and cloaks it with the opposite, calling it 'beyond sex' tenderness and intimate love." He went on to say that he thinks that her desire to drink blood is somehow linked with her need for her mother's milk and nurture, which she didn't receive.

It's interesting to look at vampires and their choices from a psychological point of view, but with sexual vampirism especially, psychology doesn't seem to really offer much understanding. It's too easy to effectively lump together blood drinking with alcoholism and other drug abuse, eating disorders, and the many other kinds of behavior that are often blamed on not getting enough mother love.

Shannon and Sandy are living in difficult times. The emptiness they seek to fill, the craving they share, has as much to do with the very real uncertainty and difficulty of life as it does with inadequate parenting. Both are still quite young and not really aware of life's possibilities. Both are good-hearted women who would surely prefer to satisfy their hunger, their need to feel special, through knowledge, accomplishment, and love.

This is not to condone their choices, but condemnation should be carefully considered. It's not a question of good versus evil. None of the vampires in this book are evil. Some are stupid and some are crazy and should completely forget their vampire fantasies and go straight into therapy. But, considering the huge variety of customs and practices found in various cultures around the world, everything from eating raw sheep's eyeballs to binding feet to shaving half of one's head as a voodoo initiate to mixing the ashes of one's cremated relative into the daily bread, is blood drinking really so strange and terrible?

It depends. With the exceptions of Shannon and Sandy, for whom blood drinking is an extension of sexual intimacy, none of the vampires in this book are really getting what they think they're getting from the blood, not nutrition, not preservation of youth, not closeness and understanding of other people, not fellowship, and certainly not power. They did get attention but, not surprisingly, the healthiest of them wanted the attention the least, agreeing to be interviewed because they were curious about others like them, not because they wanted the supposed validation of being interviewed by an author.

It's important not to romanticize the darker impulses of vampires. Many, probably most, people who drink blood do so because, confused by the books and movies, they believe it will somehow empower them, make them sexy, youthful, and beautiful. As the stories in this book show, it doesn't. When the cape is removed, a human being, flawed and confused, now with blood running down her chin, is underneath. If she was unattractive and uneducated, she still is. If he was lonely and unhappy, he still is.

The desire to drink blood may be rooted in an ancient race memory. Awareness of the urge seems to come very early in life, at puberty at the latest, with a few exceptions. Perhaps this strange desire really is something certain people are born with. Yet, time and taboos layered upon more taboos have led to the labeling of blood drinking as sick and depraved in most religions and cultures. Perhaps it is. These modern-day vampires feel passionately that it is not.

SELECTED VAMPIRE ORGANIZATIONS AND PUBLICATIONS

Vampire Information Exchange Newsletter
P.O. Box 328
Brooklyn, NY 11229-0328

If you're looking for a vampire, a good place to start is the *Vampire Information Exchange Newsletter*. For the past eight years, *VIEN* has been reliably published by Eric Held, who charges $15 a year for the quarterly publication. Some newsletter publishers take your money and never send you anything; that won't happen with Eric. In the front of each issue, new members have an opportunity to describe their specific interests, and publish their addresses, if they wish. The membership is broad: from a teenage girl with a crush on Frank Langella, to a man in the Chicago area who practices self-mutilation (even to the point of self-cannibalism), to simple horror-film buffs, to actual practicing vampires. Make your check payable to Eric Held.

> Sean Manchester
> International Society for the Advancement of
>   Irreproducible Vampire and Lycanthropy
>   Research
> P.O. Box 542
> Highgate, London N6 6BG
> United Kingdom

To order a copy of the illustrated, hardcover edition of Sean Manchester's book, *The Highgate Vampire*, published by Gothic Press, 1991, send £25 (English pounds sterling only), which includes postage, payable to Gothic Press, P.O. Box 542, Highgate, London N6 6BG, England. You can also request information about becoming a member of the society and receiving his newsletter, *The Cross and the Stake*.

> Count Dracula Fan Club
> 29 Washington Square West
> Penthouse North
> New York, NY 10011

The Count Dracula Fan Club is most appropriate for fans of vampire films and literature, although Jeanne Youngson does research in other areas of vampirism, which is sometimes described in the *CDFC News-Journal*, as well as various publications published by CDFC. Membership costs $50 for the first year, $30 a year thereafter. Members receive a DracPac, which contains a wide variety of Count Dracula Fan Club books and publications, and a subscription to the

CDFC News-Journal. Query for information about the contents of the current DracPac and other membership benefits—they change. Members visiting New York City also can arrange for a private viewing of the Dracula Museum, President Jeanne Youngson's wonderful collection of Stoker first editions, vampire memorabilia, and even a couple of Oscars won by her late husband, Robert J. Youngson, the pioneer of comedy compilations, for documentary shorts.

The Anne Rice/Vampire Lestat Fan Club
P.O. Box 58277
New Orleans, LA 70158-8277

This organization is for Anne Rice fans. For $10, you get quarterly newsletters, which provide news and updates on Anne Rice's vampire works, a membership card, and access to a pen pal program.

The Velvet Vampyre
(Carole Bohanan)
9 Station Approach
Couldson, Surrey CR3 2NR
United Kingdom

Carole publishes an extremely attractive journal called *The Velvet Vampyre,* which contains new member information, articles, short fiction, poetry, book reviews, and Carole's exquisite artwork, which is alone worth the price. Send her an international money order for £14 for a year's air-mail subscription.

Bill T. Miller
P.O. Box 221
Boston, MA 02123

Bill T. Miller, producer, musician, and owner of Immortal Records, has produced a song entitled "Blood Lust," which is based on this book. It may be the first song ever based on a book and it is certainly the first song ever written that contains samples of actual interviews done by the author. Fans of experimental rock music may recognize Miller's name—he's the founder of Out of Band Experience, on whose album *Call Now! 1-800-OUT-BAND* Carol Page also appears. If you're interested in getting a copy of "Blood Lust," the song, send $3 to the address above. Overseas readers should send a $5 international money order.

gothic
298 5th Avenue, Suite 295
New York, NY 10001

gothic is a wonderful mail order place that offers marvelous jewelry and clothes. They have everything from a men's 18th-century waistcoat to gargoyle statues to the nicest classic gothic cape I've ever seen. Prices are moderate to high. Ask to be put on their mailing list by writing to the address above.

BIBLIOGRAPHY

AA Illustrated Guide to Britain's Coast. London: Drive Publications, 1984.

Alva, Walter. "The Moche of Ancient Peru: New Tomb of Royal Splendor." *National Geographic,* June 1990.

American Psychiatric Association. *Diagnostic and Statistical Manual of Mental Disorders.* Third edition, revised. Washington, D.C.: American Psychiatric Association, 1987.

Barber, Paul. *Vampires, Burial, and Death: Folklore and Reality.* New Haven: Yale University Press, 1988.

Bohlen, Celestine. "Romania's AIDS Babies: A Legacy of Neglect." *New York Times,* February 8, 1990.

Dresser, Norine. *American Vampires: Fans, Victims, Practitioners.* New York: Norton, 1989.

Hillyer, Vincent. *Vampires.* Los Banos, Calif.: Loose Change Publications, 1988.

Hopkins, Jerry, and Danny Sugerman. *No One Here Gets Out Alive.* New York: Warner Books, 1980.

Hoyt, Olga. *Lust for Blood: The Consuming Story of Vampires.* New York: Stein and Day, 1984.

Hurwood, Bernhardt J. *Passport to the Supernatural: An Occult Compendium from All Ages & Many Lands.* New York: Taplinger Publishing Co., 1972.

———. *Vampires.* New York: Quick Fox, 1981.

Jarvis, Sharon, ed. *True Tales of the Unknown, Vol. II: The Uninvited.* New York: Bantam, 1989.

Keane, Stevan. "Light on the Darkness." *City Limits,* February 5–February 11, 1990.

Klinger, Eric. *Daydreaming: Using Waking Fantasy and Imagery for Self-Knowledge and Creativity.* Los Angeles: Jeremy P. Tarcher, 1990.

Manchester, Sean. *The Highgate Vampire.* London: British Occult Society, 1985.

Markman, Ronald, M.D., and Dominick Bosco. *Alone with the Devil: Famous Cases of a Courtroom Psychiatrist.* New York: Doubleday, 1989.

McCully, Robert S. *Jung and Rorschach.* Dallas: Spring Publications, 1987.

McNally, Raymond. *A Clutch of Vampires.* New York: Warner Books, 1975.

———. *Dracula Was a Woman.* New York: McGraw-Hill, 1983.

McNally, Raymond, and Radu Florescu. *Dracula: A Biography of Vlad the Impaler 1431–1476.* New York: Hawthorn Books, 1973.

Oke, Isiah. *Blood Secrets: The True Story of Demon Worship and Ceremonial Murder.* Buffalo: Prometheus Books, 1989.

Tannahill, Reay. *Flesh and Blood: A History of the Cannibal Complex.* New York: Stein and Day, 1975.